THE SECRET
BY
SEYMOUR LESSANS

The Secret

Seymour Lessans

Published by Safeworld Publishing Company, 2022.

ISBN: 978-1-954284-06-7 (Epub)

ISBN: 978-1-954284-12-8 (Paperback)

ISBN: 978-1-954284-17-3 (Adobe PDF)

Safeworld Publishing Company

Table of Contents

TO ALL MANKIND

A NOTE TO THE READER

THE SECRET was the author's 5th attempt to demonstrate a scientific discovery that has the power to prevent what no one wants: war, crime, and many other evils plaguing mankind. Very few people, when first reading Chapter One, which follows, will believe these changes possible. However, mathematical proof is undeniably established as the text is read chapter by chapter in the order it was written. It is important that you refrain from opening the book at random, as this would be equivalent to trying to understand a mathematical equation with the first half missing.

The problem of responsibility, the problem of reconciling the belief that people are responsible for what they do with the apparent fact that humans do not have free will because their actions are causally determined, is an ancient and enduring philosophical puzzle. This longstanding conflict in the free will/determinism debate has caused a rift in philosophical circles, which makes this perplexing conundrum appear insolvable. It is important to bear in mind that definitions mean nothing where reality is concerned unless they are reflective of reality. This is a crucial point since the reconciliation of these two opposing thought systems (while proving determinism true and free will false) is *THE SECRET* that opens the door to a world of peace and brotherhood.

Before starting, I would like to clarify a few things. The author used dialogue as a way to make the book as reader-friendly as possible, since these concepts may feel foreign at first. Also, be aware that he used humor in his writing as a form of comic relief. This should not detract from the seriousness of the subject matter. The word God is used throughout the book, which is a metaphor for the laws that govern our universe. This is not a religious work. I would also like to clarify his use of terminology. For example, the words 'mathematical' and 'scientific,' in this context, only mean 'undeniable' and are interchanged throughout the book. In the chapter on marriage, there is some sexually explicit language. This is an adult book and therefore should not be read by anybody who may be offended.

The author described his discovery as a two-sided equation, although it has nothing to do with math per se because it doesn't involve numbers. Throughout the book, he uses the phrase "*compelled, of his own free will,*" which may sound contradictory at first blush. The expression, "of his own free will," is used in a colloquial sense, which only means that he was not being coerced or forced to do anything <u>against</u> his will. It does not mean his will is free. You will understand this much better as the text is read chapter by chapter. For those familiar with this topic, this knowledge has nothing to do with compatibilism, so please don't jump to premature conclusions. When the 20th century is mentioned, this was the time the author lived. Sadly, he passed away in 1991 at the age of 72 before he was able to see his discovery brought to light. Although some examples are outdated, the discovery itself couldn't be timelier. The prediction that this new world would become a reality between 1975-1980 was based on the conviction that a thorough investigation would have already taken place.

Unfortunately, there has been no such investigation, and this discovery remains in obscurity.

INTRODUCTION

"What was so urgent, Larry, that you had to see me right away?"

"I can't stand it any longer, Jim. I feel that if I don't tell somebody real soon about what I have discovered, my mind will crack."

"Don't tell me you've discovered a pot of gold or how we can make a fortune in a short time."

"I have discovered... I don't know how to tell you this without arousing the highest degree of skepticism. Well, here goes anyway. I have discovered that the long-awaited Messiah (the solution to all problems of human relations) is nothing other than a psychological law of man's nature that has remained hidden, like atomic energy, until now. It was hidden so successfully behind a camouflage of ostensible truths that it is no wonder the mental development of our present age was required to find it. But by discovering this well-concealed law and demonstrating its power, a catalyst, so to speak, is introduced into human relations that compels a fantastic change in the direction our nature has been traveling, putting a permanent end to all war, crime, prejudice, hate, and all the other evils. Very few people are going to believe this possible."

"You don't say. And you were worried about arousing my skepticism. So, this is the big mystery? You know... you sound like some kind of nut."

"Just a minute. Isn't it true that the government of the United States is trying to find a solution to war, and don't you hear almost every day of various things being tried to reduce the number of crimes? If what I am claiming is so ridiculous or impossible, as you imply, why do we pay out billions of dollars in taxes for that very purpose — to solve our problems? If the President made an announcement that a discovery had been made, as I did, would you discount it?"

"I'd call him a crackpot, too, and me a bigger one if I believed him."

"No, you wouldn't. But because it is me, someone you are close with, someone you have known all your life, someone you might feel doesn't have the capacity to make such a discovery, you discredit the whole idea, right?"

"Well, assuming that you did make a fantastic discovery, why bring it to me? You should run to the nearest university so it can be acknowledged. Then you will be acclaimed a genius and become famous the world over."

"That's exactly what I did, but when one professor heard my claims, he smiled and lost all interest. Another used a method for screening out the wrong applicants for such a discovery. He asked from what university I graduated, and when I told him none, and that I had only gone to the seventh grade, he said... 'And you dare to come in here with such ridiculous claims about solving all the problems of human relations!' I couldn't believe my ears, and my blood was beginning to boil. In turn, I asked him from what university he graduated, and when he said Harvard, with the highest honors, I couldn't restrain myself. 'Well, tell me,' I said, 'with all your formal education, your honors, degrees, and diplomas, what discoveries have you made for the benefit of all mankind?' I wasn't really angry, just annoyed."

"I'll bet his face got red with that question."

"He didn't know what to say. But did you ever hear of anything so insulting, as if a discovery could not be made unless someone graduates college first? Isn't this a perfect example of putting the proverbial cart before the horse? After that, I was completely frustrated."

"But you must be a little sympathetic. If the universities could reject Gregor Mendel in the 19th century because his ideas on heredity disagreed with their own, it doesn't surprise me that they should reject you when your claims are so fantastic."

"But he received posthumous recognition, which should be a lesson to all professors that they should never become so dogmatic about their theories or opinions that they won't take the time to investigate anything that might lead to the truth."

"They have their own problems. Why should they spend their time solving yours? Anyway, isn't your discovery a theory?"

"I made two discoveries, and both are scientific, undeniable facts; but how can I bring this knowledge to light when the universities reject the possibility without checking it out? I even became desperate enough to phone a Catholic priest for an appointment, and our conversation went like this:

"What did you want to see me about?"

"Father, when you utter the words of the Lord's prayer, I take for granted that you are sincere and would like to see us delivered from evil, isn't that true?"

"Certainly. What kind of question is that?"

"Well, the reason I had to ask is because I have just made a scientific discovery that will bring about the actual fulfillment of this prayer, this deliverance from evil.'

"What's that you say! Deliver mankind from evil!? Absolutely impossible; it cannot be done!"

"But how can you know without first finding out what it is I have discovered? Isn't this your fervent wish that God perform such a miracle?'

"It is."

"Well then, why don't you let me come out and show you exactly how all evil must decline and fall as a direct consequence?"

"It's impossible; that's why I'm not interested. The only time such a world will become a reality is on Judgment Day."

"But that's just the point. This Judgment Day, when interpreted properly, has actually arrived because it conforms with the basic principle."

"This still doesn't convince me that I should devote my precious time to what sounds ridiculous."

"Sounds can be deceiving. Who believed the first astronomer when he predicted an eclipse, or Einstein when he revealed the potential of atomic energy? It is only natural for you to be skeptical, Father, but this is never a sufficient reason to exclude the possibility of a scientific miracle."

"I'm afraid I will have to end this conversation. My advice is to take what you have to one of the secular universities. I'm sorry I couldn't be more helpful, but thanks for calling, anyway."

"Do you see what a problem I have, Jim? I can't convince these people to give me the time, even though I have made discoveries that will benefit all mankind. That's why I just had to talk to you or else go out of my mind."

At this point, Jim began to realize that a golden opportunity had just arisen whereby he could get even with Larry at last. He never forgot how he had been hustled — trapped might be a better word — into believing that he could win at a particular game of pool, provided the odds were right. He was spotted the eight in nine-ball, and all he had to do was drive either one at any time to the back rail on a good hit. He even experimented with the balls before deciding. When finally convinced he had a good game, Larry made him understand that he would have to lay some kind of odds. By asking for 2 to 1, he was able to get 8 to 5, and they played the best out of a possible 21 games. After losing sixteen hundred and only winning two games, one of which was on the break, he realized he had been taken, but good. Later, he found out that the odds for his caliber of player to win (he was capable of running a rack of nine balls, but Larry had already run ten consecutive racks) were like ten to one. "Boy," he thought to himself, "would I like to beat him out of at least ten thousand, and now is the time. He really believes he made some kind of fantastic discovery, but he sounds like he went off his rocker. Yet I don't want to seem too anxious."

"You did the right thing by coming over, but I hope you don't think you've convinced me to devote the time. There are a lot of crack... I mean people around who are also making these claims, so you're not alone. In fact, shortly after Hitler had slaughtered 6 million Jews, I heard about a prophecy made many years ago that sometime during the 20th century a Golden Age would commence, something on the order of what you're talking about, but I laughed with contempt because I see human nature for what it is. Did your conscience bother you after beating me out of that sixteen hundred?"

"You gambled and lost, so either stop complaining or stop gambling. I didn't put a gun to your side. You're what they call a sucker, and if you're not careful, somebody might really take you."

"I know you won't. Anyway, as I was saying, these people who prophecy that the 20th century is the time for the Messiah to return might be right. In fact, you yourself might be the guy, although I doubt it."

The great humor here was that Larry knew his friend was dying to make a wager and planned to trap him into betting his life's savings — $50,000, a much greater figure than Jim had in mind. But to do this, he had to make him really think he had gone a little loco and get him angry enough.

"That's just the point; I am the Messiah."

"Come to think of it, you do look like Christ, and he was Jewish too. I don't think I would bet too much that you are not the Messiah. Maybe a wee five grand. No, that's too much for you."

"Who said so? I might even be persuaded to bet more, but you're too chicken. You like to save your money."

"Make it easy on yourself, but let me make sure I heard you right. I understand you to say that you are going to put a permanent end to all war, crime, and all the evils of human relations; is that right?"

"I said no such thing. I am going to demonstrate how two discoveries will eventually produce this great transition.

THE SECRET

I am not predicting when it will become a reality, except that all war must end between 1975 and 1980."

This last statement convinced Jim that his friend was a little meshuga.

"You talk big, Larry, but I'm tired of listening to all this bullshit. I'll see what heart you have. I'll bet ten grand you can't convince me of what you just said your discoveries will accomplish. Well, Big Shot, now what do you have to say? Either put up or shut up."

Larry played his cards very carefully, and he pretended for a fleeting moment to be afraid. But he knew that once they shook hands on a bet, it was a bet, because Jim would never back down. So, for a full two minutes he didn't say anything, as if he were trying to make up his mind. Finally, when Jim got impatient and said again:

"Well, Big Shot . . ."

He answered...

"If you're so certain I can't do this, why such a small amount? You've always been a penny-ante poker player, and you always will be. You don't have any of what I call real heart; that's your problem. But I'll tell you what I'm going to do, Big Gambler. I'll bet 50 grand that I can convince you of my claims. I happen to know you have this much stashed away in the bank."

Jim was taken completely off guard. His heart started to pound. This was his life's savings. He planned to buy a new house he had dreamt about and wanted to pay three-fourths of the cost with this money. If he lost, his wife might not only divorce him; she might shoot him. And yet he knew there was no way he could back down now. Even though he made up his mind to bet, he felt that Larry was bluffing. "I saw him do this once when some hustler asked to play a game of straight pool for $500."

'I'll play you one for $5000. I don't want to go to the table for less.'

'You've got a bet. Post.'

'Hey, this guy is serious. I was only testing to see if you had any money.'

"This has to be it," he kept thinking to himself.

"He's bluffing, but I still have to call his hand; otherwise, I'll never live it down. Besides, there is no way he can win this bet. He has to convince me that all war must end between 1975 and 1980. He just might get lucky. It could end and then start right up again in 1981."

"By the way, it could just happen that war might be at a temporary standstill at that time and have nothing to do with your discoveries."

"I am going to convince you that my discoveries will put a *permanent* end to the possibility of further wars."

Jim had no choice now but to bet, but because he felt insecure, he wanted the reassurance of someone to bet with him. He thought of Charlie, who held the most for the other bet. Besides, he is a Ph.D., and Jim needed someone like him on his side. "I'm sure he would bet at least ten thousand when he hears Larry's claims."

"Do you care if Charlie bets something and listens in on your proof?"

"I don't care if you bring the Queen of Sheba."

THE SECRET

"I know he's a gambler and that he would be interested. Suppose he should want to bet ten grand or more; what's your limit?"

"One million dollars."

"He doesn't have that kind of money. Not everybody got lucky like you did in playing the stock market."

"He can bet what he wants."

"Wait just a minute while I call him: Hi Charlie, this is Jim. Listen, something just came up that's very, very important. I won't tell you what it is on the phone, but we have an opportunity to make a lot of money. Is it all right if I come over right now?"

"Hold on a second. Alice (Charlie's new girlfriend), what time are you leaving?"

"Just as soon as I get dressed. My husband is due home in less than two hours, and I want to make sure I'm there. I haven't told him about us yet because I would rather get the divorce without involving you. He has a horrible temper. So let's just keep it this way for now. We're both having fun, right?"

"I do love you though, Sweetie, and I want you to know that I'll marry you just as soon as you get your divorce. Let yourself out, Doll. I'm talking to Jim. Yeah, Jim, you can come on over."

"Larry, you're absolutely sure now that if I can raise a million dollars, you will cover it?"

"You heard me. The trouble is everybody's chicken."

"Don't be too cocksure of that. Anyway, I'm going over to Charlie's. I'll call you later at your home."

"You sure got here fast. What's up?"

"You just won't believe what I'm going to tell you. You know Larry. Well, I think he's gone completely off his rocker, but I'm really not sure."

And then he proceeded to tell him the entire story up to date.

"By the way, how far did he go in school?"

"Only to the seventh grade, but what difference does that make?"

"It makes all the difference in the world. With my background, I can tell you now that his claims are impossible, and I'll show you how to make a complete fool out of him. The real problem is how to raise the million bucks — I mean $930,000 — since I have 20 grand myself. I have an idea. I know someone who is very wealthy. He's worth at least one billion dollars, and he respects me very much because of my education. If I can convince him that Larry's claims are really the ravings of a lunatic and there is no way he can lose, he would probably put up the difference and pay us 30%. This would give us 279 thousand to divide, plus our own winnings."

"Why do we have to put up anything?"

"This guy isn't that stupid. We must show him that we are willing to bet all that we have; otherwise, he would think something is phony. But I will still have to convince him that I know what I'm talking about. He has a big estate, is retired, and told me that I could come out to see him anytime. He's a helluva nice guy. I'm sure he's home because he never goes anywhere. So let's go.

"What's his name?"

THE SECRET

"John Tippton Howard. He's known to give millions, tax-free, to almost anybody, provided that where it came from was kept a secret. Anyway, we should be there in half an hour....... There's his big house. Just look at the size of it! It looks like a castle. The first thing we must do is ring this bell, which contacts his gardener. Here he comes. Hi! Would you tell Mr. Howard that Charlie is here to see him on urgent business?"

"Just a moment...... You may go up."

"Hi there, Mr. Howard, it's nice to see you again. I want you to meet a very good friend of mine. This is Jim Snassel. Anyway, I have something of immense importance to discuss with you."

And he related the entire story.

"Even if I should lose this money, it wouldn't bother me in the least, but you can't afford to lose your life's savings, either one of you."

"That is just the point. There is no way he can win. He only went to the seventh grade in school, and believe me, I'll make a fool of him."

"Do you know this person, Larry, very well, Jim?"

"I grew up with him."

"Could you tell me something about him before I invest this money? I realize that Charlie is very proud of his education, but you see, I, too, never finished high school. However, this is no criterion, and we are not discussing making money, and I do respect Charlie's education. He is a brilliant person. But no man is willing to bet one million dollars unless he is either off his rocker, as you express it, or else he might really have something. Therefore, I would like to determine this for myself, so do you mind if I ask a few questions?"

"Not at all."

"Is he good at anything?"

"He's one of the best pool players in the country."

"Besides that."

"When he was six years old, he showed enormous talent at the piano, and when he was thirteen, he played chess exceptionally well."

"But Mr. Howard, that doesn't mean anything where education is concerned."

"I'm not arguing with you, Charlie. What else was he good at?"

"He was extremely fast on his feet. When we played football, basketball, or softball, he was always the one everybody wanted on their side. He used to walk along and do front flips on the sidewalk without touching his hands on anything. His gym teacher told him that he could become a master tumbler if he practiced."

"That doesn't mean anything regarding education."

"He's a whiz at mathematics. In fact, he has one problem that no professor has ever worked out. I couldn't even understand the question. He gave Charlie this problem. Did you ever work it out?"

"No, I didn't, but that's different. It has no bearing on this. Just remember, I have a tremendous background in history, psychology, philosophy, and science. I'm more aware than he will ever be of what human nature really is. My professor was a master psychologist."

"Did he ever do much reading?"

THE SECRET

"I remember he liked The Decline and Fall of the Roman Empire by Edward Gibbon."

"Did you ever read that book, Charlie?"

"Only excerpts. It wasn't necessary to read it all. Besides, later historians proved he was incorrect in many things."

"Did Larry finish reading this work? Although I never read it, I heard it was a tremendous undertaking."

"I thought he would never stop reading it. He read it at least seven times completely. He also read The Story of Civilization by Will Durant many times. He read innumerable philosophers, books on medicine, a great deal of literature. I remember that he used to get up at six in the morning and read until he left for work, which was at eight thirty. He would read on the bus going, during his lunch hour, on his way home, and after dinner for two hours, always carrying a dictionary. In fact, he wore out five of them, so he told me. He tried to get me interested in acquiring this liberal education, but it had no appeal. He read like this for 15 years. When he came out of the service, I remember he took a test to find out what kind of job he should train for. He told me that five professors called him in for an interview because they couldn't believe the results of the test. His intelligence quotient was the highest they had ever seen. He had a vocabulary that put theirs to shame. And when he asked them what he qualified to study, he was told that he would succeed at anything he undertook."

"But he's still not a Ph.D. The more I listen to Jim, the more I'm convinced he really went off his rocker. Imagine implying that he's the Messiah."

"Charlie, he might not be the Messiah, but his education appears to be much greater than you care to give him credit for. Therefore, in view of the fact that you were basing this investment on your ability to show him up, or on his being slightly crazy, I'm afraid I will have to forgo this kind of opportunity. Thanks for coming out, fellows. Call me at any time."

They left in a state of disappointment.

"Listen, Jim. I'm going to get together another 20 grand by borrowing it. This will give us ninety thousand. Believe me, he can't do what he said. 'A permanent end to all war?' That's ridiculous!"

"I should have asked him what month."

"Don't you start acting nutty. Call him up right now and tell him that we will draw our money out tomorrow. Tell him that we will deposit the 180 thousand in a joint account that will require three signatures. Do you think he will object to that? After all, we could refuse to sign our names."

"I thought you were so certain he couldn't win. Why even discuss that possibility?"

"It's just a figure of speech. Now listen, I'm off for the next two weeks."

"I can take off."

"You make all the arrangements. We'll plan to meet at my place. Yours is too noisy with the kids and your wife around. Today is Wednesday; I'll give you my money tomorrow, and we should be all set by Friday morning. If there is any change, let me know; otherwise, I'll expect both of you at my place with the bankbook on Friday at 9 a.m., and don't worry about the money. You'll see how I trap him."

THE SECRET

They each went their own way, and on Friday morning, they met at Charlie's apartment.

"Come on in, fellows! Hi, Larry. I haven't seen you since that pool match with Jim. I see you have the bankbook. Boy, you sure are carrying a lot of notes, or is that a manuscript?"

"A manuscript."

"There's some coffee on the stove, if you want any."

Jim and Larry went in to get some, and when they came out, they noticed that Charlie had opened the manuscript to the middle, and as he was reading, he began to smile.

"Listen, Charlie, my problem is difficult enough as it is without having you jump to premature conclusions as a result of what you just did. Kindly leave my manuscript alone."

"I didn't mean to offend you, but I was curious. After all, the claims you have made are fantastic."

"You're betting ninety thousand dollars between you to see my hand, right? So let me show it to you."

"Before you do, I have a very important question. You made the statement that you discovered two things, so Jim told me, whatever they are, and you refer to them as scientific. Now, just supposing your scientific discoveries contravene other scientific discoveries, how are you going to determine who is right?"

"If this should occur, and I'm not saying it will, then it is obvious that certain scientific facts are not scientific, either mine or the others."

"But won't you need someone who is not betting to sit in on this, someone qualified to determine whether yours is just an opinion?"

"You mean someone who will judge my hand according to what he has been taught. This won't be necessary because we already have an expert sitting in, someone absolutely infallible. His name is — Undeniable Mathematical Relations. Let me explain what I mean by asking you this question. If it is mathematically impossible to prove something true, whatever it is, is it possible to prove the opposite of this something false?"

"Larry and his logic."

"This has nothing whatever to do with logic, Jim. This is pure, unadulterated mathematics. Well, what is your answer?"

"I think it is possible."

"I was directing my question more to Charlie."

"But I disagree with him. You see, we already have a disagreement. Charlie is right. We do need someone to sit in on this who is an expert."

"We already have an expert, Jim. Charlie's answer was correct, and your answer was incorrect only because you didn't see the undeniable mathematical relation, so let me rephrase the question so you can see the relation. If it is mathematically impossible to prove something true, whatever it is, is it possible to prove this something true?"

"Now I get it. By asking if it is possible to prove the opposite of this something false, you were actually saying the same thing."

"Do you need a professor to tell you that this is true, and that it is not a matter of opinion? Do you need an expert to tell you that 3 is to 6 what 4 is to 8, and that this is also not a matter of opinion?"

THE SECRET

"No, but I have heard of some people who claim that nothing can be proven true."

"I am not interested in these people, only in the two of you, and if we can't have a solid basis for communication, then there is no point in going any further. Now, do either of you disagree that two plus two equals four, or would you rather chicken out and call the bet off? This is your privilege."

"I'm not backing out for anything; how about you, Jim?"

"I'll go all the way, even if I get shot by my wife, so continue."

"Now do you understand that only undeniable mathematical relations will be used?"

"So you say."

"Consequently, anything that contains within itself proof of its veracity does not require the long tenure of an accepted belief, theory, scientific misconception, or the high rank of a formal education, such as yours, as a standard of qualification for the truth, right?"

"I told you once, we agree."

"But supposing I can't follow the reasoning that you say contains this proof of its veracity, what then? Some people can't understand why 3 is to 6 what 4 is to 8."

"We are not discussing some people. You are the ones I have to convince, and if I can't, you win."

"For this amount of money, I might suddenly discover that 2 plus 2 equals 5, and you might not be able to convince me otherwise."

"If that should happen, wise guy, and there is disagreement, then I will let you select any three people you want, who know nothing about the bet, to determine who is right. Is that fair enough?"

"You can't be fairer than that."

"The fact that you mentioned what you just did, Jim, presents a certain amount of ironic humor. Because you are interested in winning this money, you certainly would not like to see the relations that will put an end to all war; isn't that true? Would you, Charlie, like to see an end, through these relations, to all crime, hate, prejudice, and evil in general if this would cost you 40 grand?

"You're right. I want to win at all costs. But if I were the one responsible for causing this evil by winning the bet, then I could not enjoy seeing millions of people made to suffer for this amount of money."

"Could you enjoy it for a price? Hitler did. He wanted to rule the world, and for this power, he was willing to pay any price, such as slaughtering 6 million Jews."

"Not me, and I doubt if Jim could. But what has this to do with that ironic humor you mentioned?"

"Let me show you what I mean. How happy would the medical profession be if one morning 98% of all the patients in the world called up their doctor to tell him this: 'Hi Doc, guess what? I have the greatest news to tell you. Something happened overnight, as if by miracle. Don't ask me what; I don't know. I just want to say thanks for everything, but I won't be needing your services anymore. Send me my final bill.' How excited and thrilled will all governments and religions be to learn that their services to fight against the evil in our lives will soon no longer be required because the very things for which these forces came into existence will be prevented from arising or continuing? Is it not obvious that doctors would be extremely happy when all sickness is removed? Isn't it obvious that priests would much rather see an end to all sin than to preach against it and shrive the sinners in the confessional; that politicians, statesmen, the leaders of the world in general would much rather see an end to all war and crime than to retaliate an 'eye for an eye and a tooth for a tooth'?"

"There is a fallacy with your ironic humor. I agree that they should be happy for the welfare of mankind, but they couldn't be pleased to have taken away the source of their income and the very things that gave meaning to their existence. A salesman is happy to make a sale when he works on commission, but if he found out that another salesman beat him to the punch, he would be disappointed, even though the person buying derived whatever benefit was in the object sold. There are two things involved, and earning a living cannot be overlooked. In other words, the doctors are sincerely interested in making their patients well, but they want to be the ones to do it. Theologians would like to see us delivered from evil, but in some manner that takes them into consideration. The Chinese government would like to see this new world, but in terms of communism or socialism. Everybody would like to see a great change. 'I have a dream,' said Dr. Martin Luther King (this view from the mountaintop), but no one desires any intruders or interlopers."

"I agree with you, Charlie. But if all the people in the world who get displaced only because their services are not needed anymore, were to know, as a matter of undeniable knowledge, that the income necessary to sustain their standard of living, whatever the cost, would never be stopped as long as they live, would they have any reason to complain about someone showing them a better way, the only way to accomplish that for which they are being paid?"

"I can't see any, but of course, this is a hypothetical question."

"Would you complain, Jim?"

"Only if it costs me 50 grand."

"Well, I've got good news for both of you. I'm going to show you how you can't lose your money, yet you could still win my ninety thousand. You see, you are judging that I don't have the solution based upon your present understanding of human nature and the fact that it seems impossible. Go back two centuries, and landing men on the moon was thought to be an impossible dream. How many times in the course of history has the impossible (that is, what seemed impossible) been made possible because of scientific discoveries? However, just because there were never any comparable discoveries in the field of psychology up until now doesn't mean there will never be any, and this is where I've got both of you by the balls. I can actually see that this new world must become a reality as a direct consequence of my two scientific discoveries when they are extended into human relations; therefore, I am prepared to do something if I am wrong (but remember, I know I am right), that you should be willing to do if you are wrong, but remember, you can't be positive that you are right because you don't know what I have discovered."

"What in the hell are you talking about?"

THE SECRET

"I'm going to bet my ninety thousand dollars, not against your ninety (you can keep your money; I know you need it), but against your right hands. In your kitchen, I saw a meat cleaver. Now, if I can't convince you that I am right in my claims, you will not only collect my ninety grand, but you can chop off my right hand at the wrist. On the other hand (this might be the only one left if you win), should you be the loser, I will have the right to chop off both of your right hands. Now you don't have to accept this bet, but if you do and lose, you at least will still have your money, although you might not shoot pool too well afterwards. Well, Big Gamblers, what's it going to be?"

"You're absolutely crazy! Of course, we won't go for that just because you say it's true; we don't know what you have. Let me remind you that many people before you have been equally positive that they were right about something, only to be proven wrong. Maybe Charlie's Ph.D. degree will bet his right hand, but I can't risk mine."

"Just because he's willing to make such a bet does not mean that he's proven anything. And remember why Socrates was considered the wisest man of his time. He said, 'I know that I don't know, whereas others don't know either, only they think they know.' Isn't it possible that you just think you know?"

"Isn't it possible that you just think I don't know? Socrates knew that he didn't know, whereas I know that I know that I know that I know. As for people being positive about something only to be proven wrong, if you look closely, you can see the fallacious standard hidden in your reasoning: Because others were positive and wrong, I could be wrong because I am positive. But Edison was positive and right. Einstein was positive and right. The scientists who planned a moon landing were positive and right. The first astronomer who observed the mathematical laws inherent in the solar system, which enabled him to predict an eclipse, was positive and right. The reason Jim was willing to make the wager was not because he felt this new world was an absolute impossibility, but he did not think it possible for me to have made such a discovery because he was judging me by fallacious standards, by the fact that I am his friend and therefore couldn't possibly have made a discovery that will change the world; while you, Charlie, were weighing my 7th grade education."

"I must admit that your confidence in being willing to bet your right hand has me a little worried at this point, but the most that could happen is the loss of my life's savings. At least I will have a consolation prize — this new world — but my wife might not appreciate it."

"He's got a long way to go to win our money. Well, am I allowed to ask for my forty grand — what are your discoveries? Can you explain them in a few words?"

THE SECRET

PART ONE
THE FOUNDATION AND DEVELOPMENT OF
TWO SCIENTIFIC DISCOVERIES

CHAPTER ONE
THE FIRST SCIENTIFIC DISCOVERY

"In order for me to win the bet, it is absolutely necessary that I de-confuse your mind. Therefore, I shall not even attempt to explain anything in a few words, although I will be as brief as possible."

"What was so terrible about my opening your manuscript in the middle?"

"Didn't you read something that seemed impossible, which made you smile incredulously? The first four chapters must be studied thoroughly before any other reading is done, not only because they are the key that will unlock this door to the greatest treasure in the history of mankind (the long-awaited GOLDEN AGE that has been hoped and prayed for since time immemorial), but also because the rest of the chapters, though much easier, will not make any sense otherwise. Whereas others might find these four chapters a little difficult even after studying them thoroughly, for which they shouldn't get discouraged because what follows will help them understand it much better the second time around, I will make absolutely sure you guys won't have any trouble whatsoever, not for one hundred and eighty thousand dollars.

Incidentally, when you have finally grasped the full significance and magnitude of these discoveries (it took me ten years to figure out this tremendous mathematical equation), and I have collected, which allows you to receive your consolation prize (a copy of this book — free — so it can remind you of this happy occasion), you will realize there has never been, and will never be, another like this one, and you will treasure it throughout your entire life."

"He sounds like we already lost."

"Well, what's the first step?"

"I shall let you see what these two discoveries are and how they are related to man's ultimate nature, something you have never been aware of; and then, after you thoroughly understand the basic principles involved, that is, after I am finished with the four chapters, I shall extend these discoveries into the world of human relations, and several fantastic miracles will follow just as naturally and smoothly as the earth revolves on its axis."

"Why did you call them miracles? Will they transcend the laws of nature?"

"They will not."

"Are you claiming that God will perform them, not man?"

"That's absolutely true, Charlie. I didn't want to bring this out just yet, but the two discoveries allow God to reveal himself for the very first time to all mankind in an undeniable manner."

THE SECRET

"That's what I wanted you to admit. I resent your bringing God into this at all. I don't go for all that religious crap when you're talking about science. Jim likes religion, but I can't stand all this ritual and mumbo jumbo. Most people who go to church are hypocrites anyway. Besides, I know you never believed in religion either, never went to the synagogue, and never prayed to God. In fact, you even mocked those who did, more than me. I say again, I resent this."

"Jim, take note that Charlie has just conceded the bet."

"I did no such thing."

"Well, why are you telling me how I should go about presenting my scientific discoveries? And why are you always jumping to conclusions? Is this what they taught you in college? Now remember, anytime you don't like how I present my case, you can leave, but this is equivalent to resigning in chess when you can't win. In order for me to show you how these so-called miracles come about, you must let me do it my way. Is that asking too much, or am I being unreasonable?"

"I'm sorry, Larry, and I apologize. Continue."

"The fact that I never went to the synagogue or prayed is equivalent to my not desiring to do other things that didn't interest me. However, my criticizing those who did perform certain rituals was only an expression of my unconscious ignorance. But when I made my discoveries, I knew for a fact that God was not a figment of the imagination. Plato, Christ, and many others came very close to the truth, but the element of evil was always an unsolved factor. Spinoza said evil was not evil when seen in total perspective, which was a true statement, but since this made God the first cause and responsible for everything, he allowed his sister to cheat him out of his inheritance because he refused to blame her. Christ did the same thing, and when they nailed him to the cross, he was heard to say, 'They know not what they do.' How was it possible for him to blame them when he knew that they were not responsible? 'Turn the other cheek,' he said. But Will Durant, not at all satisfied with this aspect of Spinoza's philosophy, although he loved him dearly, could not understand how it was humanly possible to turn the other cheek in this kind of world. And he was right. Didn't the Bible say, 'an eye for an eye and a tooth for a tooth?' Why was the mind of man so confused, and why, despite every possible criticism, was religion able to convince the world to be patient and have faith? Where did these theologians receive their inspiration, since there was no way science could reconcile good and evil with a God that caused everything? They solved this problem by dividing good and evil in half, and God was only responsible for the first. Is it any wonder that Christ and Spinoza, plus innumerable others, pulled away from the synagogue, just as I did? Is it any wonder Spinoza became a heretic and was excommunicated? Is it any wonder that you, Charlie, react as you do towards religion? How can any intelligent person believe in Satan? Since the modern world of science was playing hell with religion, it needed a boost and along came, just in the nick of time, a scientist who gave seven reasons why he believed in God. A. Cressy Morrison, who wrote his book Man Does Not Stand Alone as a challenge to Julian Huxley's conclusions who titled his book Man Stands Alone, was almost convinced that God was a reality. His arguments were mathematically sound, and he gave quite a boost to instilling faith again in those people who were really beginning to wonder. I can almost remember word for word how he tried to prove that nothing happens by chance, and he did prove it, except for this element of evil. It went something like this:

'Chance seems erratic, unexpected and subject to no method of calculation, but though we are startled by its surprises, chance is subject to rigid and unbreakable law. The proverbial penny may turn up heads ten times in a row and the chance of an eleventh is not expected but is still one in two, but the chance of ten heads coming up consecutively is very small. Suppose you have a bag containing one hundred marbles, ninety-nine black and one white. Shake the bag and let out one. The chance that the first marble out being the white one is exactly one in one hundred. Now put the marbles back and start again. The chance of the white coming out is still one in a hundred, but the chance of the white coming out first twice in succession is one in ten thousand (one hundred times one hundred).

Now try a third time, and the chance of the white coming out three times in succession is one hundred times ten thousand or one in a million. Try another time or two and the figures become astronomical.

The results of chance are as clearly bound by law as the fact that two plus two equals four.

In a game in which the cards are shuffled and an ace of spades was dealt to one of the players, ace of hearts to the next, clubs to the third and diamonds to the dealer, followed by the deuces, the threes and so on, until each player had a complete set in numerical order, no one would believe the cards had not been arranged.

The chances are so great against such a happening that probably it never did happen in all the games played anywhere since cards was invented. But there are those who say it could happen, and I suppose the possibility does exist. Suppose a little child is asked by an expert chess player to beat him at chess in thirty-four moves and the child makes every move by pure chance exactly right to meet every twist and turn the expert attempts and does beat him in thirty-four moves. The expert would certainly think it was a dream or that he was out of his mind. But there are those who think the possibility of this happening by chance does exist. And I agree, it could happen, however small the possibility.

To repeat, my purpose in this discussion of chance is to bring forcibly to the attention of the reader the fact that the purpose of this book is to point out clearly and scientifically the narrow limits which any life can exist on earth, and prove by real evidence that all the nearly exact requirements of life could not be brought about on one planet at one time by chance. The size of the earth, the distance from the sun, the thickness of the earth's crust, the quantity of water, the amount of carbon dioxide, the volume of nitrogen, the emergence of man and his survival — all point to order out of chaos, to design and purpose, and to the fact that, according to the inexorable laws of mathematics, all these could not occur by chance simultaneously on one planet once in a billion times. It could so occur, but it did not so occur. When the facts are so overwhelming, and when we recognize, as we must, the attributes of our minds which are not material, is it possible to flaunt the evidence and take the one chance in a billion that we and all else are the result of chance?

We have found that there are 999,999,999 chances to one against a belief that all things happen by chance. Science will not deny the facts as stated; the mathematicians will agree that the figures are correct. Now we encounter the stubborn resistance of the human mind, which is reluctant to give up fixed ideas. The early Greeks knew the earth was a sphere, but it took two thousand years to convince men that this fact is true.

The argument is closed; the case is submitted to you, the jury, and your verdict will be awaited with confidence.'

But Morrison never realized that all the mathematical arguments in the world could never reveal God until we were delivered from evil; consequently, he was compelled to join the ranks of those who had faith. Nobody has yet said he knows for a mathematical fact that God is real; otherwise, there would be no need for faith. I know that two plus two is equal to four. I don't believe or have faith that this is true."

"I get the whole picture now. Your discoveries, whatever they are, will deliver mankind from evil and prove conclusively that God is a reality."

"That's true, but the evil is not removed to prove that God is not a figment of our imagination, but only because it is evil. He becomes an epiphenomenon of this tremendous fire that will be built to burn away the evil, and the light that is shed reveals his presence as the cause of the evil that he is now removing through my discoveries, which he also caused, and no person alive will be able to deny it."

"Hey Charlie; and he only went to the seventh grade. Show him up, kid. Show him how smart you are."

"Don't be funny. Well, when are you going to reveal your first discovery?"

"In just a few minutes. Now, one of the most profound observations ever made was by Socrates, who said, 'Know thyself,' but though he had a suspicion of its significance, it was only an intuitive feeling, not something he could put his finger on. These two words have never been adequately understood by mankind, including psychiatry and psychology, because this expression is the key that will unlock the first door to another door, which requires its own key. Well, are you ready?"

"Are you kidding?"

"Before you start..."

"Jesus Christ, Jim, did you have to? I'm dying to find out what this first discovery is already. What is so important?"

"It just occurred to me that it is mathematically impossible for God to be a reality because there is no way perfect justice can prevail. Look at all the people who have suffered and died to develop this world, and won't be around when the fruit of their labor has ripened to maturity. Do you call this justice?"

"I meant to tell you, but there was no immediate rush. I actually made three mathematical discoveries, not just two, and the last one is going to give you the greatest and most pleasant surprise in your life. But it has nothing to do with the removal of evil as such. Don't try to guess because you never will, since you are compelled to use words like metempsychosis, reincarnation, an afterlife, etc., and these mean absolutely nothing unless you are able to extract the pure, unadulterated mathematical relations that are involved. Can you be patient, Jim? Remember, I can't explain everything at one time, and I must proceed in a manner that brooks no opposition."

"I don't mind waiting."

"Now Charlie, what is the meaning of the word epistemology?"

"Don't tell me you're going to show me that the sun exists in my head, not in the sky."

"Why do you always jump to conclusions, and the wrong ones? I asked you a simple question. If you don't know the answer, just tell me."

"I'm not familiar with the exact definition, but it has to do with the theory or science of the method and grounds of knowledge, especially with reference to its limits and validity. But all our knowledge is derived through our sense organs."

"And how many senses do we have?"

"Are you trying to be funny? Five, naturally."

"Now let me ask what might appear, on the surface, to be a ridiculous question. Are there any people in the entire world who believe that man does not have five senses?"

"Are you referring to that so-called sixth sense, this extra-sensory perception?"

"Why do you always assume you know what I'm going to say? I don't mean that at all."

"Well then let me answer you this way. It is possible that somewhere in the world someone exists who believes that man does not have five senses, but the odds are greater than what Morrison pointed out. Since I don't know of anyone, I would say that everybody believes — not believes but knows that this is an accurate scientific observation. Do you agree, Jim?"

"I do, but are you trying to tell us, Larry, that man does not have five senses?"

"That's right; he does not. This originated with Aristotle and has never been analyzed thoroughly."

"But what difference does it make what we call them? The substance of which they are made is still the same."

"It makes all the difference in the world. There was a time when man believed the earth was flat, and though it is true his opinions can never change the actual shape of the earth, how could it have ever been possible to land men on the moon without first knowing that the earth is a sphere? In other words, this belief in the flatness of the earth prevented scientific investigation by closing a door to all those who believed it. Consequently, if everybody knows that man has five senses when in reality he does not, how is it possible for anyone to open the door marked Man Does Not Have Five Senses?"

"He's right, Charlie. In a million years, I would never think to open that door. But why don't we have them?"

"Because the eyes are not a sense organ. Aristotle made an assumption that they functioned like the other organs, and he called all of them senses. This is equivalent to calling an apple, pear, peach, orange, and potato five fruit. Since we can see that the potato is not a fruit because it is grown differently, there isn't any problem, but when you learn what this single thing (believing or knowing the eyes are a sense organ) has done to the world of knowledge, you won't believe it at first. But before I open this door marked Man Does Not Have Five Senses to show you all the knowledge hidden behind it, it is absolutely necessary to prove that the eyes are not a sense organ.

The dictionary states that the word sense is 'any receptor, or group of receptors, specialized to receive and transmit external stimuli, as of sight, taste, smell, etc.' But this is a wholly fallacious observation where the eyes are concerned because nothing from the external world impinges on the optic nerve as stimuli do upon the organs of hearing, taste, touch, and smell."

"Hold it just a minute! I have been taught by science, and I repeat, science, that light travels approximately 186,000 miles per second, and that the light from the sun takes roughly 8 minutes to reach us. These light waves strike the optic nerve and allow us to see the sun and all other things. I also remember reading that if we could sit on the star Rigel with a very powerful telescope focused upon the earth, we would just be able to see the ships of Columbus reaching America for the first time. Are you trying to tell us that these are not scientific facts?"

"Are you positive because you were told this, or positive because you, yourself, saw the relations revealing this truth? And if you are still positive, will you put your right hand on the chopping block to show me how positive you really are?"

"I am not that positive, but we were taught this."

"It is accurate that light travels at a high rate of speed, but the other observations are completely false. So, without further delay, I shall prove something never before understood by man. Now tell me, Charlie, did you ever wonder why the eyes of a newborn baby cannot focus?"

"I understood from a doctor that the muscles of the eye are too weak at this early age."

"And he believes this because he was taught that, but it is not the truth. In fact, if a child at birth was placed in a soundproof room with his eyelids removed and kept alive for 50 years, if possible, on a steady flow of intravenous glucose without allowing any stimuli to strike the other 4 organs of sense, this baby, child, young, and middle-aged person would never be able to focus the eyes to see any objects existing in that room, no matter how much light was present or how colorful they might be, simply because the conditions necessary for focusing the eyes have been removed, and there is nothing, absolutely nothing, that travels from an object, including the light from the sun, that causes it. This can be scientifically tested."

"But doesn't light cause the pupils to dilate and contract, depending on the intensity?"

"That is absolutely true, but this does not cause; it is a condition of sight. We simply need light to see."

"Do you agree with this, Charlie?"

"I don't agree or disagree yet because he hasn't shown us what does cause the eyes to eventually focus."

"This takes place for the first time when sense experience (hearing, taste, touch, and smell — these are doorways in) awakens the brain, which then focuses the eyes so that the child can look through them, as binoculars, at what exists around him. The eyes are the windows of the brain through which experience is gained, not by what comes in on the waves of light that strike the optic nerve, but by what is looked at in relation to sense experience. This is an efferent experience, the other an afferent experience. In other words, if we on earth were living in total darkness because God had not yet turned on the light of the sun, but we knew that he planned to flip the switch at 12 noon, it would remain dark for 8½ minutes until the light has reached us after traveling at a high rate of speed. But once the light is here, the photons, emitted by the constant energy of the sun, continue to surround us. When the Earth rotates on its axis so that the section on which we live is in darkness, this only means the photons of light are on the other side. When our rotation allows the sun to smile on us again, this does not mean that it takes another 8½ minutes for this light to reach us because these photons are continually being produced by the Sun's energy. And if the sun were to explode while we were looking at it, we would see it the instant it happened, not 8½ minutes later. The reason we are able to see the moon, the sun, the distant stars, etc., is not because one is 3 seconds away, the other 8 minutes away, and the last many light-years away, but simply because these objects are large enough to be seen at their great distance when enough light is present. To put this another way and paraphrase your quotation: 'If we could sit upon the star Rigel with a very powerful telescope focused upon the earth, we would be able to see the very same things going on right now that everybody else sees. This fallacy has come into existence because the eyes were considered a sense organ like the ears. Because it takes longer for the sound from an airplane to reach our ears when it is five thousand feet away than a thousand, it was assumed that the same thing occurred with the object sending a picture of itself on the wings of light."

"But if it were possible to transmit a television picture from the earth to a planet as far away as the star Rigel, is it not true that the people living there would be seeing the ships of Columbus coming into America for the first time?"

"That is absolutely true, Charlie, because the picture is being transmitted through space at a certain rate of speed. But objects do not send out pictures that travel through space and impinge on the optic nerve. We see objects directly by looking at them, and it takes the same length of time to see an airplane, the moon, the sun, or distant stars. The scientists did the same thing Aristotle did. He assumed the eyes functioned like the other four, and they assumed he was right, which made all their reasoning fit what appeared to be undeniable. How else was it possible for knowledge to reach us through our eyes when they were compelled to believe that man had five senses? Were they given any choice?"

"I agree with him, Charlie. Everything he says makes sense; the other way does not."

"I agree also, but I can't see where this is such a terrific scientific discovery, and I can't see any relation at all between this and the removal of all evil."

"This is only the key to unlock the door. As for your being unable to see the relation, that is because you are only a P.hD., I mean Ph.D. (I was pronouncing it incorrectly), whereas I, with all my reading, studying, and thinking, am a Ph-Ph-Ph-Ph-Ph-Ph.D. You only went to the 20th grade in formal school, but I went to the 120th grade in informal school, so I am six times more educated than you. I'm only having a little fun, Charlie, and this is really not a criticism. The whole world will be laughing as well as crying from happiness very shortly when they see the tremendous humor of this fantastic transition and realize that God fooled everybody. But he directed me to the solution, and that's the only reason I found it. Please don't misunderstand my words. You will know what I mean soon enough. Let us now open wide this door and see what lies behind it."

SEYMOUR LESSANS

CHAPTER TWO
WORDS, NOT REALITY

"Maybe Charlie's degree doesn't entitle him to ask this question, but I would like to know why we have been able to develop so many scientific achievements without ever knowing the true function of the eyes."

"Simply because this misconception didn't prevent us from extracting the pure mathematical relations that led to these other scientific achievements, except in the case of the person who made the observation on the star Rigel. However, let me make one thing absolutely clear: I couldn't care less about distance having no effect on the time it takes to see things, but I am very much concerned with the removal of all evil, which is symbolic of any kind of hurt that exists in human relations. Consequently, since this is related to specific words that have come into existence and are not descriptive of reality, although they appear to be, the next step is to reveal them and why they have caused more unhappiness and hurt than can be readily imagined."

"But I have been taught to believe that 'sticks and stones will break my bones, but names or words will never hurt me.' Isn't that a true statement?"

"He's not referring to those names, Jim."

"I'm not. To be called the N word, kike, dirty Jew, Chink, wop, pig, or any name used in an effort to make you feel inferior is actually not a hurt because you know that this does not lower yourself in your own eyes. You allow for the source. But when you are judged an inferior production of the human race by others as well as yourself, all because of words that have no relation to reality — although you see this inferiority as if it is a definite part of the real world — then you are seriously hurt, and I am going to put a permanent end to the use of these words."

"Let's assume for the moment that you actually convince us that these words are a hurt, why should we, or others, stop using them if there is greater satisfaction in continuing with them? People are taught that it is wrong to steal, commit adultery, and murder, but this doesn't stop these and other things. By the same reasoning, teaching us that using certain words, whatever they are, is wrong because they hurt people, won't necessarily stop their use."

"You are one hundred percent right, Charlie, but I am not going to demonstrate, at this point, how these will come to an end because this involves my second discovery when it is extended. So, without further ado, let me show you what these words are and why they are not in any way symbolic of reality."

"But you made a statement that is already false because I don't consider myself inferior to anybody, except in certain things. I know you are a better pool player than me, and in that regard, I am inferior to you, but this can never make me feel that I am an inferior production of the human race."

THE SECRET

"This can't, I agree, but something else can. Since you have no more money to bet and you need your hand, let me show you what I mean. Do you consider your girlfriend as beautiful as Elizabeth Taylor, or yourself as handsome as Robert Taylor was?"

"I had an idea that this was what he was driving at, but he made a slip, Jim. He'll never win our money this way. Now tell me, how is it possible to answer your question when beauty is in the eyes of the beholder? This is just a matter of opinion, not a fact, and you said that these words were symbolic of reality or gave the appearance of being so."

"Are you so positive you know whereof you speak that if I spot you with my two hands to your one, you would unhesitatingly make this bet?"

"He always stops me with that, Jim. No, I am not that positive."

"Well, let me show you how confused your mind is by rephrasing my question: In your eyes, do you consider Alice as beautiful as Elizabeth Taylor?'

"No, I don't."

"In your eyes, is this an opinion that you are less good-looking than Robert Taylor was, or a fact?"

"He was an extremely handsome man, and I do consider him better-looking than myself."

"Do you, Jim, consider your wife as beautiful as Elizabeth Taylor?"

"I wish she were. Boy, would I like to get... Never mind, I'll only work myself up."

"Who do you consider better looking, Marlon Brando or Elvis Presley?"

"The latter."

"Not in my book. Brando had it all over him."

"Now, are you able to see what the expression 'Beauty is in the eyes of the beholder' refers to? There is a difference of opinion as to who is more handsome in your eyes, but once you admit to yourself that a certain person is prettier than another, then, as far as you're concerned, this is not an opinion but a fact. Take a look at this picture. It is of a girl who has an aquiline nose, heavy bowlegs, sagging breasts, a projected rear end, a harelip, and who lisps and stutters. Now compare her with Elizabeth Taylor and tell me the truth. In your eyes, which one is more beautiful?"

"Are you trying to be funny? Elizabeth Taylor, naturally. But this is a fact: she is more beautiful. These differences exist and are a definite part of the real world because I see them with my very eyes."

"Differences exist; this is true, and you do see them with your very eyes, but the words we have been looking through are not, and because these symbols are a terrible hurt, they must come to an end. God is giving us no choice, as you will soon see. However, the first thing I must do is demonstrate exactly why they are words only, not reality; otherwise, you will classify this kind of evil as one of those unfortunate things, like being born without legs, arms, or eyes. Now, to help me explain what I mean, let us return to a baby and watch how he learns words.

By constantly hearing certain sounds in relation to specific objects, he soon knows that apple, orange, doll, dress, sun, moon, dog, cat, mommy, daddy, etc., mean the very things he sees with his eyes. These bits of substance are a definite part of the real world, and he knows this even before learning the words. He has experienced most of these with his four senses, and even though this cannot be done where the sun and moon are concerned, he still sees that something is there. Remember, however, that nothing from the external world strikes his optic nerve to allow him to see these various objects. He simply sees these things because he looks at them. A dog also sees these objects because he looks at them. He tastes, smells, and hears various things, but since nothing strikes his optic nerve, he must confirm what he is doubtful of with his sense of smell. In other words, if a vicious dog, accustomed to attacking any stranger who opened the back gate even in broad daylight, were to have his sense of hearing and smell disconnected, he would have amnesia and attack his own master if the gate was opened because he would have no way of knowing that this person was not a stranger since nothing is striking his optic nerve to reveal anything familiar."

"But doesn't the brain take a picture through the eyes of the differences that exist? I can see them through my eyes; why can't a dog see them through his?"

"Because he knows nothing of differences. He enjoys certain toys more than others. He likes his master and dislikes strangers. He likes to eat certain foods, mate with particular females, but there is no way his brain can perceive differences because this involves words. Let me show you what I mean.

A baby also sees objects, but when he learns orange, pear, apple, sun, moon, daddy, mommy, he soon learns that these bits of substance are different, and that is why they have different names. The word mommy is a picture of all the differences that separate her from others, and when the baby looks at her through this symbol, all the differences are seen because this word is equivalent to a slide or negative plate in a movie projector. If a picture of mom flashed on a screen, the child would automatically say mommy. But a dog cannot identify his master from any kind of picture because nothing from the external world impinges on its optic nerve, causing it to recognize the differences. But the baby is able to identify mommy because the word is a picture that was taken when the relation was formed and exists in the mind of the child, through which he looks at the differences that exist in substance. As he looks through a book, he says, 'cat, dog, cow, goat,' etc., but only because he has these word-slides or negative plates existing as a relation in his mind. However, if some kind of accident disconnected these slides from their relation with each other, then he would have amnesia and would not be able to recognize his own mother because she would appear to him as a total stranger. This also proves conclusively that a tremendous number of people classified as colorblind are actually word blind. In other words, if a child is able to see all the differences in colors even before learning all the words, then he is not colorblind and will never get confused. But if he does not learn the words properly, then he can very easily get mixed up over differences. But this observation is really not important. Let us now see what happens when we learn the words beautiful, adorable, cute, pretty, etc.

As these words constantly ring in our ears, a picture is again taken of these differences in substance, and just as a child will say dog when seeing a certain four-legged animal, he will also say pretty dog, pretty dress, pretty baby, pretty girl, which separates, in his mind, the differences between these things that evoke the use of the word pretty and those that do not. He sees that a bulldog is not called by this name, nor is a rat. He sees that the girl next door is not called cute, and she sees this too, and he knows these differences are real because he sees them with his very eyes, with direct perception. At first, he doesn't hear the words ugly and homely, but it doesn't take long for him to know that these differences belong to those who never get called pretty, cute, etc. Now let me show you how man was able to do the impossible as a result of words. He was actually able to stratify the differences in people into layers of value when it is mathematically impossible for anything of value to exist in the external world."

"I'm afraid to say anything, but aren't food and money of value, and don't these exist externally?"

"They exist externally, but their value is strictly in relation to you. An animal cannot say this food or female is better because it cannot project a value into substance, which requires words. But when a word contains a judgment of value, a standard of perfection, then we are able to project this value directly into substance, and then, because we see this with our very eyes, it was a simple thing to convince ourselves that beauty was a part of the real world. To understand this a little better, let us resort to a movie projector.

Here is a smooth white wall in a dark room with nothing on it. I am dropping this negative plate or slide into the projector, flipping the switch, and just take a look — there is a picture of a girl on the wall. But go up and touch her. All you feel is the wall itself. There is no substance. Now we have been doing the exact same thing with our brains regarding values."

"Where in the hell did you dig up all these things?"

"If I were to tell you how I came to make my discoveries, you wouldn't believe it, and one day I might just tell the story. But I was given no choice. God directed me every step of the way, and he kept buzzing in my ear that all war must end between 1975 and 1980. I was confused at first, but he wouldn't let up until I was not confused. Now he smiles at me and says, 'I told you.' It took him better than ten years to de-confuse my mind, but I can de-confuse yours in less than a week."

"Why do you predict only war to end by then? Why not crime?"

"To end any particular evil (and you are in for so many surprises) requires that the people involved understand the principles that will be explained. When they do, they will be given no choice but to stop the evil, whatever it is they are engaged in. But whereas it is only necessary to get the leaders of the world to understand the principles to end all war, it takes all mankind to understand them to put a permanent end to crime. Believe me, your consolation prize will be worth more than your ninety grand."

"Well, then why don't you give it back if we lose?"

"This is God's payment to me for my ten years of work. If you don't like it, take it up with him. He's my boss."

THE SECRET

"I'm beginning to feel that we made a bad bet. How was I to know that your friend Larry had the capacity to think like this? I was misled when you told me he only went to the 7th grade."

"It was the truth. My wife used to admire his ability to do so many things perfectly that one day she remarked, 'Just imagine what he might have accomplished had he gone to college.' I believed her, and I really had confidence in your Ph.D. degree. So don't blame me if we lose."

"Take it easy, fellas; you haven't lost yet. We have a long way to go. Anyway, to get back on track, the differences in substance were not only divided up by the use of words such as apple, dog, etc., but substance itself became a screen upon which we were able to project this value. But drop a negative plate in your brain projector and flip the switch. Well, just take a look; there is now a beautiful girl, a homely man, an ugly duckling! Turn off the switch (remove the negative plate or word slide), and all you see are the differences in substance because the projected values have been removed. Since we were taught that the eyes receive and transmit sense experience on the waves of light, it was impossible for us to create in our imagination what was striking the optic nerve; consequently, it was impossible to deny that this beautiful girl was a part of the real world. And when we changed the standard hidden in the word, all we were doing was changing the screen. By saying this person may not be beautiful physically, but she has a beautiful soul, we were allowed to see this other standard as if it, too, existed externally. How many times have you heard someone remark, 'It's a shame she got killed. She was such a pretty girl, too.' This demonstrates that the girl killed contained a greater value because of this prettiness. Why are you smiling, Charlie?"

"Because you are right. But this knowledge will never get rid of these words... I mean, I don't think it is possible, but I'm not absolutely sure."

"That's much better. I am positive, however, and I will bet all my money, any part of my body, or my life that I will get rid of these words. Can you imagine what would happen if we lived in a world where all such words were removed, where nobody, including ourselves, would be judging us in terms of ugliness, homeliness, prettiness, etc.? We have been handicapped from the day of our birth because we were compelled to look at each other through a kaleidoscope of words that transformed us realistically into what we were not. Every other word we use stratifies external differences, which cannot be denied, into fallacious values that appear realistic because they are seen with the direct perception of our very eyes. Why else do people get their teeth squeezed together, nose jobs, and do any number of things, if not to make themselves more beautiful? But you are in for the surprise of your life very shortly because if any reader of my book, when I finally get it published, starts out with a feeling of superiority or inferiority, I will guarantee that when he understands all the principles, and he will, he will end up feeling exactly equal with every person alive, no better or worse. God is really wonderful, and you ain't seen nothin yet."

CHAPTER THREE
THE WILL OF MAN

Realizing that man could destroy himself unless there were forces to control his nature during the years of development, God created, along with everything else, religion, which, in spite of everything, was a bright light in the story of civilization. However, in order to reach this stage of development so he could reveal himself to all mankind by performing this deliverance from evil, it was absolutely necessary to get man to believe his will was free, and he confused the mind to such a degree that 98% of all mankind believed in this theory, consciously or unconsciously. It became a dogma, a dogmatic doctrine of all religion, was the cornerstone of all civilization, and the only reason man was able to develop. Now, because of its extreme importance, I shall repeat this statement. Man could never have developed had it not been for his belief in free will, consciously or unconsciously. However, there were those who came into the world and saw the truth, but in a confused sort of way. Jesus Christ was one, and when he told the rabbis, as Spinoza did, that God commanded man to turn the other cheek, they threw him out because the Bible told them that God said, 'an eye for an eye and a tooth for a tooth.' But because he exemplified in his behavior certain principles, and because he saw such suffering in the world, he drew to himself those who needed help, and there were many. However, the legacy he left for Christianity was never reconciled. How was it possible to turn the other cheek in a world of such evil? Theology solved this in a very simple manner by claiming that God endowed man with the ability to choose good or evil. This absolved God of the responsibility for evil, which was assigned to Satan, but it never reconciled the two principles, 'an eye for an eye and a tooth for a tooth,' with 'turning the other cheek.' And when Will Durant came along, he, as well as many philosophers, helped the cause of free will using syllogistic reasoning in a completely unconscious sort of way. He asked himself, 'How is it possible not to fight back when hurt?' and he was one hundred percent correct, which compelled him to write: 'If there is an almost eternal recurrence of philosophies of freedom' (free will), 'it is because direct perception can never be beaten down with formulas, or sensation with reasoning.' He was trying to say in this sentence that philosophies of free will would never stop returning just as long as our nature commands us to fight back when hurt, but this is not what he actually said. What he meant to say was absolutely undeniable because this relation could be seen just as easily with direct perception as two plus two equals four, and there was no way that this statement could be beaten down with formulas or reasoning. But to come right out and say that two plus two equals four when 98% of the world knows this would be foolish, and to set up this undeniable relation syllogistically would also be foolish because then we would have something like this: 'If there is an almost eternal recurrence of' four equaling two plus two, 'it is because' two equals one plus one, and one plus one plus one plus one totals four. So instead, he tried to prove freedom of the will by demonstrating that determinism could never prove it false by unconsciously using the same type of syllogistic reasoning. He made this his major premise: direct perception is superior to reasoning in determining the truth. He made his minor premise: free will is not a matter of reasoning, like determinism. Then he concluded: since philosophies of free will employ direct perception, which cannot be beaten down by the reasoning of determinism, the belief in free will must return almost eternally. He knew that free will was a theory, but as long as proof was not necessary when it could be seen with the direct perception of our common sense that it was impossible to turn the other cheek — the corollary thrown up by determinism — he was compelled to write: 'Let the determinist honestly envisage the implications of his philosophy?' And the amazing thing is that both sides of this equation are correct. Christ said, 'Turn the other cheek,' and Durant said, 'This is impossible.' Just think about this for a moment. Would you believe that both principles are mathematically correct?

"How is that possible? Can you answer that, Charlie?"

"Remember, I am only a Ph.D."

"God made the reconciliation of these two principles the time when he would reveal himself to all mankind, but to get here, you can see what had to be done first, since the paths leading up to this understanding were camouflaged with layers upon layers of words that concealed the truth."

"Why can't free will be proven true?"

"Do you want to answer this, Charlie? Never mind. Now I'm going to give you an example of pure mathematical reasoning, so tell me, Jim, is it possible not to do what has already been done?"

"Naturally, it is impossible for me not to do what has already been done, because I have already done it."

"Now, if what has just been done was the choosing of B instead of A, is it possible not to choose B, which has already been chosen?"

"Impossible, naturally."

"Since it is absolutely impossible not to choose B instead of A once B has been selected, how is it possible to choose A in this comparison of possibilities when in order to make this choice you must not choose B, which has already been chosen?"

"Again, I must admit it is something impossible to do."

"Yet free will, to prove itself true, must do just that — the impossible. It must go back, reverse the order of time, undo what has already been done, and then show that A, with the conditions being exactly the same, could have been chosen instead of B. Since it is utterly impossible to reverse the order of time, which is absolutely necessary for mathematical proof, free will was compelled to remain a theory until now. But to show you how confused the mind can get when mathematical relations are not perceived, pay close attention to this: Even though it is mathematically impossible to prove free will true, which means that it is also mathematically impossible to prove the opposite (determinism) false (because this would prove free will true), yet Durant wrote: 'For even while we talked determinism we knew it was false.' The reason theologians could never solve the problem of evil was simply because they never looked behind the door marked, Man's Will Is Not Free. Why should they open it when they were convinced man's will is free? Spinoza opened it and looked around quite a bit, but he did not know how to slay the fiery dragon, so he pretended it wasn't even there: "Evil is really not evil when seen in total perspective. But we are men, not God." Durant also went in and looked around very thoroughly, and he, too, saw the fiery dragon, but unlike Spinoza, he made no pretense of its nonexistence. He just didn't know how to overcome the beast, but he refused to agree with what common sense told him to deny. This dragon has been guarding an invisible key and door since time immemorial, and this could never be made visible except to the prince who slayed him. I'll never forget how, in November of 1959, God first called me for the job. I happened to overhear on the radio a priest say very dogmatically that man has freedom of the will, and the hair stood up on my arms like a cat ready to fight. I didn't pay much attention to it at the time and felt that I was chilled for some reason. But when it occurred every time the subject came up, I saw the connection and decided to read once again Will Durant's chapter on free will. This is all I will tell you right now. However, after slaying the dragon, I saw a sign that read: 'Hidden behind this door, you will discover the long-awaited Messiah, the solution to all problems of human relations.' I applied the key, opened the door, and saw how this new world must become a reality in a very short time."

"Is proving that man's will is not free the key to open the door and your second discovery?"

"Of course not. I just told you that the fiery dragon must be killed to get the key. First, I must prove that man's will is not free so we can come face to face with the fiery dragon, and I will prove it in a mathematically undeniable manner. Then I shall jab him in the right eye, then the left; then I shall cut out his tongue (I took fencing lessons for this job), and finally I shall pierce him in his heart. Then, when I have made certain he is dead..."

"I thought you killed him already."

"I did, but there is a dragon for each person, so instead of giving everybody a sword (steel is high these days), I shall slay him so the whole world can see that he is dead. And now, let me get by the first step to accomplish this, which is to prove conclusively, once and for all, that man's will is not free.

The dictionary states that free will is 'the power of self-determination regarded as a special faculty of choosing good and evil without compulsion or necessity. Made, done, or given of one's own free choice; voluntary.' But in reality, we are carried along on the wings of time or life during every moment of our existence, and we really have no say in this matter whatsoever. We cannot stop ourselves from being born or getting older, and are compelled to either live out our lives as best we can or commit suicide. Is it possible for either of you to disagree with this?"

THE SECRET

"I understand and agree so far, don't you, Jim?

"I do."

"However, to prove that what we do of our own free will, of our own desire, because we want to do it, is also beyond control, it is necessary to employ mathematical (undeniable) reasoning. Therefore, since it is absolutely impossible for man to be both dead and alive at the same time, and since it is absolutely impossible for a person to desire committing suicide unless dissatisfied with life, we are given the ability to demonstrate a revealing and undeniable relation.

Every motion, from the beating heart to the slightest reflex action, from all inner to outer movements of the body, indicates that life is never satisfied to remain in one position for always, which shall be termed death. I shall now call the present moment of time or life — here, for the purpose of clarification, and the next moment coming up — there. You are now standing on this present moment called here and are given two alternatives: either live or kill yourself; either move to the next spot called there or remain where you are without moving a hair's breadth, which is death or here. Which do you prefer?"

"I prefer... "

"Excuse the interruption, Jim, but the very fact that you started to answer me, or didn't commit suicide at that moment, makes it obvious that you were not satisfied to stay in one position and prefer moving off that spot to there, which motion is life. Consequently, the motion of life, which is any motion from here to there, is a movement away from that which dissatisfies; otherwise, had you been satisfied to remain here, you would never have moved to there. Since the motion of life constantly moves away from here to there, which is an expression of dissatisfaction with the present position, it must obviously move constantly in the direction of satisfaction."

"You are talking to me, not only Charlie. Can you explain this in words that I might more easily understand?"

"Yes, I can. Supposing you were taken prisoner in wartime for espionage and condemned to death, but mercifully given a choice between two exits: A is the painless hemlock of Socrates, while B is death by having your head held under water. Is it humanly possible to prefer exit B if A is offered as an alternative?"

"Yes, if this meant that those I love would not be harmed in any way."

"Leave it to Charlie."

"Well, if this was your preference under these conditions, could you prefer the other alternative?"

"No, I couldn't; but you really haven't given me any alternative."

"But if your will is free, you should be able to choose B just as well as A, or A just as well as B. The reason you are confused is because the word choice is very misleading, for it assumes that man has two or more possibilities, but in reality this is a delusion because the direction of life, always moving toward satisfaction, compels him to prefer of differences what he considers better for himself, and when two or more alternatives are presented, he is compelled, by his very nature, to prefer not that one which is considered worse, but what gives every indication of being better for the particular set of circumstances involved. The purpose of choosing is to compare meaningful differences to decide which alternative is preferable. A and B, representing small or large differences, are compared. The comparison is absolutely necessary to know which is preferable. The difference, which is considered favorable, regardless of the reason, is the compulsion of greater satisfaction desire is forced to take, which makes one of them an impossible choice in this comparison simply because it gives less satisfaction under the circumstances. Consequently, since B is an impossible choice, man is not free to choose A."

"I agree with all this; so does Jim, I'm sure."

"I want him to make it a little more clear for me."

"How many times in your life have you remarked: 'You give me no choice' or 'it makes no difference.'"

"I can't count the number. But..."

"Just because some differences are so obviously superior in value where you are concerned that no hesitation is required to decide which is preferable, while other differences need a more careful consideration, doesn't change the direction of life, which moves always towards greater satisfaction than what the present position offers. The truth of the matter is that all through life, man is under a compulsion to choose what he considers good for himself, but what you may judge good or bad for yourself doesn't make it so for others, especially when it is remembered that a juxtaposition of differences in each case presents alternatives that affect choice. Now just take careful note of this simple mathematical reasoning that proves conclusively, beyond a shadow of doubt, that will is not free: Man either doesn't have a choice because none is involved, as with aging, and then it is obvious that he is under the normal compulsion of living, regardless of what his particular motion at any moment might be, or he has a choice, and then is given two or more alternatives of which he is compelled, by his nature, to prefer the one that appears to offer the greatest satisfaction, whether it is the lesser of two evils, the greater of two goods, or a good over an evil. Therefore, it is absolutely impossible for the will of man to be free because he never has a free choice."

"It's amazing, Charlie. All my life I have believed man's will is free, but for the first time I can actually see that his will is not free."

"You may be satisfied, but I'm not. Determinism is defined as 'the philosophical and ethical doctrine that man's choices, decisions, and actions are decided by antecedent causes, inherited or environmental, acting upon his character.' But I know for a fact that absolutely nothing can cause me to do what I make up my mind not to do, not even the most severe tortures or the threat of death. If I don't want to do something, nothing, not environment, heredity, or anything else you care to throw in, can make me do it, because over this I have mathematical control. Therefore, in this sense, my will is free because I can't be made to do anything against my will."

"How about that, Larry! He brought out something I never would have thought of."

"All he said was that 'you can lead a horse to water but you can't make him drink,' which is undeniable. However, though it is a mathematical law that nothing can compel man to do to another what he makes up his mind not to do (this is an extremely crucial point), he is nevertheless under a compulsion during every moment of his existence to do everything he does. This reveals, as Charlie pointed out, that man has mathematical control over the former but absolutely none over the latter because he must constantly move in the direction of greater satisfaction."

"I'm confused again, though Charlie might not be."

"In other words, no one is compelling a person to work at a job he doesn't like or remain in a country against his will. He actually wants to do the very things he dislikes simply because the alternative is considered worse, and he must choose something to do among the various things in his environment or else commit suicide. Was it humanly possible to make Gandhi and his followers do what they did not want to do when unafraid of death, which was judged the lesser of two evils? Consequently, when any person says he was compelled to do what he did against his will, that he really didn't want to but had to (and innumerable of our expressions say this), he is obviously confused and unconsciously dishonest with himself and others because everything man does to another is done only because he wants to do it, done, to be humorous, of his own free will, which only means that his preference gave him greater satisfaction at that moment of time for one reason or another."

"His reasoning is perfect, Jim; I can't find a flaw, although I thought I did."

"I think I understand now. Just because I cannot be made to do something against my will does not mean my will is free, because my desire not to do it appeared the better reason, which gave me no free choice since I got greater satisfaction. Nor does the expression, 'I did it of my own free will, nobody made me do it,' mean that I actually did it of my own free will, although I did it because I wanted to, because my desire to do it appeared the better reason, which gave me no free choice since I got greater satisfaction."

"He does understand."

"Does this mean that you are also in complete agreement, so I can proceed?"

"Yes, it does."

CHAPTER FOUR

THE SECOND SCIENTIFIC DISCOVERY

Now the belief in free will came into existence out of absolute necessity, not only to absolve God of all responsibility since he was considered good, but because it was impossible for man to solve his problems without blame and punishment, which required the justification of this belief in order to absolve his own conscience. In other words, if you, Jim, were called upon to pass judgment on someone who committed a crime by sentencing him to death or prison, could you do it if you knew his will was not free?

"I see what you mean. No, I definitely could not."

"To punish him in any way, you would have to believe that he was free to choose another alternative than the one for which he was being judged; that he was not compelled by laws over which he had no control. Man was given no choice but to think this way. But once it is established as a mathematical undeniable law that will is not free, which was just demonstrated (and here is why my discovery was never found; no one could ever get beyond this point; this is the fiery dragon), it becomes absolutely impossible to hold man responsible for anything he does."

"If the solution lies beyond this point, no wonder it was never found. How is it possible not to blame and punish people for committing murder, rape, theft, and the wholesale slaughter of 6 million Jews? Does this mean that we are supposed to condone these evils? And wouldn't man become even less responsible if there were no laws and threats of punishment to control his nature? Doesn't our history show that if he wants something badly enough, he will go to any lengths to satisfy his desire, even commit murder and pounce down on other nations with talons or tons of steel? What is it that prevents the poor from walking into stores and taking what they need and want, if not the fear of punishment? This strikes at the very heart of all civilization, the teaching of what is right and wrong, for how is it humanly possible not to blame a person for hurting others?"

"Is it any wonder that Durant turned around and retreated after looking the dragon in the eye? Is it any wonder the Jews excommunicated Spinoza and Christ? Is it any wonder religion becomes hostile towards those who even mention that man's will is not free? Supposing I called up a priest right now and told him the solution to all the problems of human relations — the deliverance of man from evil — is prevented from becoming a reality because of his belief in free will. What do you think he would say? Would he care to invite me out? Of course not, because he knows man's will is free. Now you must bear in mind that if it had not been for the development of laws and a penal code, for the constant teaching of right and wrong, civilization could never have reached the outposts of this coming Golden Age.

Yet despite the fact that we have been brought up to believe that man can be blamed and punished for doing what he was taught is wrong and evil (this is the cornerstone of all law and order up to now), the force that has given us our brains and bodies, the solar and mankind systems; the force that makes us move in the direction of satisfaction (or this invariable law of God) states explicitly, as we perceive these mathematical relations and prepare to shed the last stage of the rocket that has given us our thrust up to this point, that since man's will is not free, Thou Shall Not Blame."

"I really don't know how you plan to solve this enigmatic corollary, but it seems to me that this knowledge would give man a perfect excuse for taking advantage of others without any fear of consequences. In other words, he could just say, I'm sorry, but I couldn't help myself because my will is not free."

"Now let me show you again how really confused you are, Charlie. If someone does what everybody considers right as opposed to wrong, that is, if this person acts in a manner that pleases everybody, is it possible to blame him for doing what society expects of him? This isn't a trick question, Jim, so don't look so puzzled. In other words, if your boss tells you that he wants something done a certain way and you never fail to do it that way, is it possible for him to blame you for doing what he wants you to do?"

"No, it is not possible."

"I agree."

"Consequently, if you can't be blamed for doing what is right, then it should be obvious that you can only be blamed for doing something judged wrong. Is that right?"

"Jim and I agree to this."

"These people who are judging you for doing something wrong are interested in knowing why you could do such a thing, which compels you, for satisfaction, to lie or think up a reasonable excuse to extenuate the circumstances and mitigate their unfavorable opinion of your action; otherwise, if they were not judging your conduct as wrong, you would not have to do these things, right?"

"He's right again, Charlie."

"Now if you know as a matter of positive knowledge that no one is going to blame you for what you did, wrong or right, that is, no one is going to question your conduct in any way because you know that they must excuse what you do since man's will is not free, is it possible for you to blame someone or something else as the cause for what you know you have done, when you also know that no one is blaming you? In other words (take your time with this), is it possible to make an effort to shift your responsibility when you know that no one is holding you responsible? Why are you smiling, Charlie?"

"You're the greatest, Larry, with your mathematical reasoning. But I agree that it is not possible."

"This proves conclusively that the only time man can say, 'I couldn't help myself because my will is not free,' or offer any other kind of excuse, is if someone said he could help himself or blamed him in any way so he could make this effort to shift his responsibility, right?"

"He is absolutely right, Charlie."

"Which means that only in the world of free will, in a world of judgment, can this statement — 'I couldn't help myself because my will is not free' — be made, since it cannot be done when man knows he will not be blamed."

"Even though I cannot disagree with anything thus far, why should this prevent man from stealing more easily what he wants when the risk of retaliation is no more a condition to be considered, and how is it humanly possible for those he steals from and hurts in other ways to excuse his conduct? We are right back where we were before — the fiery dragon."

"But not for long. Now tell me, Charlie, would you agree that if I did something to hurt you, you would be justified to retaliate?"

"I certainly would be justified?"

"And we have also agreed that this is the principle of an eye for an eye, correct?"

"Correct."

"Which means that this principle does not concern itself with preventing the first blow from being struck, but only with justifying punishment or retaliation; is this also true?"

"Yes, it is."

"And the principle of turning the other cheek — doesn't this concern itself with preventing the second cheek from being struck, not the first cheek?"

"He's right, Charlie."

"Therefore, our only concern is in preventing the desire to strike this first blow, for then, if this can be accomplished, our problem is solved. If the first cheek is not struck, there is no need to retaliate or turn the other side of our face. Is this hard to understand?"

"It's very easy, in fact. I'm not a college graduate and I can even see that relation."

"Now let us further understand that in order for you to strike this first blow of hurt, assuming that what is and what is not a hurt has already been established (don't jump to conclusions), you would have to be taking a certain amount of risk, that is, you would be risking the possibility of retaliation or punishment, is that correct?"

"Not if I planned a perfect crime."

"The most you can do with your plans is reduce the element of risk, but the fact that somebody was hurt by what you did does not take away his desire to strike a blow of retaliation. He doesn't know who to blame, but if he did, you could expect that he would desire to strike back. Consequently, his desire to retaliate an eye for an eye is an undeniable condition of our present world, as is also your awareness that there is this element of risk involved, however small. This means that whenever you do anything at all that is risky, you are prepared to pay a price for the satisfaction of certain desires. You may risk going to jail, getting hanged or electrocuted, shot, beaten up, losing your eye and tooth, being criticized, reprimanded, spanked, scolded, ostracized, or what have you, but this is the price you are willing to risk or pay in order to satisfy certain desires. Well, can you disagree with this?"

"I still say, supposing there is no risk. Supposing I was able to plan a perfect crime and never be caught."

"I'm not denying the possibility, but you can never know for certain; therefore, the element of risk must exist when you do anything that hurts another."

"Then I agree."

THE SECRET

"Now pay close attention because I am about to slay the fiery dragon with my trusty sword, which will reveal my discovery, reconcile the two opposite principles — 'An eye for an eye and turn the other cheek,' and open the door to this new world.

At this present moment of time, you are standing on this spot called <u>here</u> and are constantly in the process of moving to <u>there</u>. You know, as a matter of positive knowledge, that you would never move to <u>there</u> if you were not dissatisfied with <u>here</u>. You also know, as a matter of undeniable knowledge, that nothing has the power, that no one can compel or cause you to move to <u>there</u> or do anything against your will — unless you want to — because over this, you know that you have mathematical control. And I, who am standing on this spot called <u>there</u> to where you plan to move for satisfaction from <u>here</u>, also know positively that you cannot be blamed anymore for your motion from <u>here</u> to <u>there</u> because the will of man is not free. This is a very unique two-sided equation which reveals that while you know you are completely responsible for everything you do since no one has the power to make you do anything you don't want to — and while you also know it is mathematically impossible to shift your responsibility to some extraneous cause when you know that no one holds you responsible — everybody else knows that you are not to blame for anything you do because you are compelled, by your very nature, to move in the direction of greater satisfaction during every moment of your existence. Now if you know as a matter of undeniable knowledge that not only I, who am the one to be hurt, but everyone on earth will never blame you for hurting me in some way; never criticize or question your action; never desire to hurt you in return for doing what must now be considered a compulsion beyond your control since the will of man is not free, is it humanly possible for you to derive the slightest element of satisfaction from the contemplation of this hurt? (Hold it just a moment, Charlie) Remember now, you haven't hurt me yet, and you know (this is the other side of the equation) as a matter of undeniable knowledge that nothing, no one can compel you to hurt me unless you want to, for over this you have mathematical control; consequently, your motion from <u>here</u> to <u>there</u>, your decision as to what is better for yourself, is still a choice between two alternatives — to hurt me or not to hurt me. But the moment it fully dawns on you that this hurt to me, should you go ahead with it, will not be blamed in any way because no one wants to hurt you for doing what must now be considered a compulsion beyond your control — although you know it is not beyond your control at this point since nothing can force you to hurt me against your will unless you want to — you are compelled, completely of your own free will (so to speak), to relinquish this desire to hurt me because it can never satisfy you to do so under these changed conditions. In order to hurt another, man must be able to derive some satisfaction from this, which means that he was previously hurt and is justified to retaliate (an eye for an eye), or else he knows absolutely and positively that he would be blamed by the person he hurt and others if they knew. Punishment and retaliation are natural reactions of a free will environment that permit the consideration of hurt because they are the price man is willing to risk or pay for the satisfaction of certain desires. But when they are removed so the knowledge that they no longer exist becomes a new condition of the environment, then the price he must consider to strike the first blow of hurt (all others are justified) is completely out of his reach because to do so, he must move in the direction of conscious dissatisfaction, which is mathematically impossible. The answer to this impasse, which opens the door by killing the dragon, is now very obvious because the advance knowledge that he will not be blamed or punished for the first blow of hurt since his will is not free — when he knows that nobody, nothing can compel him to hurt others <u>unless he wants to</u>, for over this he has mathematical control — enters a condition or catalyst never before a permanent factor in human relations and mathematically prevents those very acts of evil for which blame and punishment were previously necessary as a normal reaction in the direction of greater satisfaction. Now what were you going to say?"

"Something puzzles me very much because it seems that under certain conditions, this principle can have no effect. If man is compelled to move in the direction of greater satisfaction, and the conditions of the environment cause him, as a solution to his particular problem, to prefer the lesser of two evils, how is it possible to remove the evil when his choice, no matter what he selects, is still evil? In other words, self-preservation is the first law of nature, and if he can't satisfy his needs without hurting others, the knowledge that they will never blame him for this hurt to them can never prevent him from moving in this direction because he has no choice."

"You are one hundred percent correct, Charlie, because he is already being hurt by the environment, and under such conditions, he is justified to retaliate. However, how this is solved will be answered very shortly, so would you mind being patient?"

"Not at all. This is the only thing that had me puzzled; otherwise, your reasoning is flawless. But don't expect us to concede that we lost our bet at this point, even though your equation is completely undeniable to the nth degree. Do you understand it, Jim?"

"I certainly do, and I think it is marvelous, but I would like to go over everything again."

"I'm going to give each of you a copy of what was just discussed so you can study it thoroughly. However, even if you didn't grasp all the relations it wouldn't be something in your favor, simply because any doubts that may arise will be cleared up as I extend this magic elixir (call it what you will, corollary, slide rule or basic principle — THOU SHALL NOT BLAME — and transmute the baser metals of human nature into the pure gold of the Golden Age.

This new world is coming into existence not because of my will, not because I made a discovery (sooner or later it had to be discovered because the knowledge of what it means that man's will is not free is a definite part of the real world), but only because we are compelled to obey the laws of our nature. Do you really think it was an accident that the solar system came into existence; an accident that the sun is just the proper distance from the earth so we don't roast or freeze; an accident that the earth revolves just at the proper speed to fulfill many exacting functions; an accident that our brains and bodies developed just that way; an accident that I made my discovery exactly when I did? To show you how fantastic is the infinite wisdom that directs every aspect of this universe through invariable laws that we are at last getting to understand, which include the solar and mankind systems, just follow this. Here is versatile man: writer, composer, artist, inventor, scientist, philosopher, theologian, architect, builder, mathematician, chess player, murderer, prostitute, thief, etc. — whose will is absolutely and positively not free despite all the learned opinions to the contrary — yet compelled by his very nature and lack of development to believe that it is since it was impossible not to blame and punish the terrible evils that came into existence out of necessity, and then permitted to perceive the necessary relations as to why will is not free and what this means for the entire world, which perception was utterly impossible without the development and absolutely necessary for the inception of our Golden Age. Where in all of history have you ever heard anything more incredible? We have been growing and developing just like a child from infancy. There is no way a baby can go from birth to old age without passing through the necessary steps, and no way man could have reached this turning point in his life without also going through the necessary stages of evil.

"Tomorrow, after you have had an opportunity to study everything thoroughly, I shall perform some fantastic miracles, but I will not be transcending the laws of our nature. You can kiss your money goodbye."

"I'm still skeptical, but giving you the benefit of the doubt at this point, what will be your first miracle?"

"I am going to demonstrate, in an absolutely undeniable manner, that all premarital relations, adultery, and divorce must come to a permanent end in the new world, not because this is morally wrong and man has decided at last to obey the Ten Commandments, but only because the conditions that led to a heart being broken and cut out with the knife of unrequited love will be prevented from arising, making it apparent that those who lost in the game of love were very unhappy people, even though in this world it may be better to have loved and lost than never to have loved at all. The word miracle in this context will only have reference to the removal of all the factors truly responsible for preventing a boy and girl from falling mutually in love and living happily ever after. My friends, the GOLDEN AGE has arrived at last."

THE SECRET

PART TWO
THE EXTENSION OF THESE DISCOVERIES AND
THEIR PRINCIPLES,
INTO THE WORLD OF LOVE

SEYMOUR LESSANS

CHAPTER FIVE
PREMARITAL RELATIONS

"You implied that this new world, without premarital relations, adultery, and divorce, would be a better place in which to live, as if these things were evil. I can't think of anything that gives me greater pleasure than this affair I'm having with Mary. My wife doesn't know about it, and what she doesn't know won't hurt her. Besides, I still take care of my homework, and I assume Mary does too. Yet she and I make such passionate love that there is no comparison in our marriages. Frankly, if I didn't have her, I don't think I could tolerate my wife."

"I agree with Jim, although my circumstances are different. He doesn't want to divorce his wife because he wants his cake and eat it too."

"And we sure do eat it."

"But although my relationship is premarital with Mary, who is committing adultery, she wants to get a divorce; at least I think she does if her husband will give her one. She can't stand him any longer, especially since he got fat and lost what little sex appeal he had. Besides, he doesn't even know how to satisfy her, and I do. She told me there is such a vast difference between making love with me and him that you just wouldn't believe it. But judging what I see happen in so many marriages, I realize the possibility exists that she might desire to cut out on me once we make it legal, which seems to lessen the thrill and excitement of lovemaking. What's the expression? ... 'Forbidden fruit is sweet.' That's why I wouldn't want to marry Mary, because I fear the same thing would happen. I just want her body, nothing else. It's great! And here you are telling us that these things we need for our happiness are coming to an end. I don't think I would like to live in this kind of world. It's impossible... I mean, I think it's impossible to be married for any length of time and have the kind of passionate relationship that goes hand in glove with adultery. Consequently, my conclusion (I'm entitled to my opinion, right?) is this: Since sex is one of man's strongest desires, and since in adultery this desire reaches its highest peak, adultery will always be with us."

"You picked up this syllogistic reasoning very well."

"And I have to agree with him. Just as long as there are men who do not want to get married or remarried, girls who need sex but can't find the boys to make it legal, and sexually unsatisfied married couples, we will always have premarital relations, adultery, and divorce."

"And once again, you are one hundred percent correct, but the conditions are going to change. However, in order for you to appreciate this great change and for me to perform this miracle, it is absolutely necessary that you understand what causes our present environment, so let me begin by defining, in a mathematical (undeniable) manner, what we mean exactly by the word love; otherwise, we would not continue to have a solid basis for communication. It symbolizes a conscious or unconscious desire, in varying degrees, for a sexual relation of some kind, and this is easily proven by the fact that it is impossible for a boy or girl to fall in love with, or be attracted to someone no matter how physically appealing this individual might be considered, if they know in advance that this person was born without sexual organs, which knowledge makes them aware that this freak of nature is incapable of giving or receiving sexual satisfaction."

"I agree with that because I know if a girl didn't have the very things that give me such tremendous satisfaction, I couldn't be drawn to her no matter what her face and figure were like."

"This means that before sexual intercourse takes place, the degree with which one could fall in love is determined by the degree with which the desire to possess a particular person in the ultimate act, as in marriage, is encouraged. But the meaning of love after marriage or sexual intercourse takes place is a horse of another color, for the intensity of this desire to continue possessing the other depends solely on the degree of sexual satisfaction, which proves conclusively that the stronger the passion, the greater will this feeling of love be and further demonstrates why there are so many divorces, so much adultery, and so many broken hearts. Most couples remain together after physical satisfaction has sunk to its lowest ebb, not because they are still in love (desire a sexual relationship with each other except as a last resort), but only because it is the lesser of two evils when children, money, and adultery are involved. However, before I demonstrate the first stage of the solution, let us see how this problem arises by observing two boys meeting two girls for the first time.

"You told me some cute girls were going to be at this dance, Charlie. All I see are a bunch of bags. Wait... just... a... minute! Look at what just walked through the door, and she has a girlfriend with her. Let's rush right over before some other guys see them. I'll take the girl on the left, you know, the gorgeous one.'"

"Supposing she prefers me?"

"Not a chance, Buddy Boy, and you know it. But the other one isn't half bad on a rainy night. Hi Honey! My name is Jim. This is Charlie. We saw you come in and rushed right over to ask for a dance. What's your name?"

"Mary. This is Jane."

"How about it, Mary? Would you like a 'trip to the light fantastic'?"

"I sure would."

"Boy... you really follow me great! You're a very attractive girl, but I don't have to tell you that. I'm sure you must have heard it many times before. How about after the dance, all of us get soda, and then we'll take you and Jane home?"

"I don't mind. I'm sure Jane won't."

At the door, Jim and Charlie asked them for a date, and they accepted. Now, when a boy and girl start dating, they are compelled to look at each other through words or slides that not only place them somewhere on the scale of physical perfection but transform them realistically into what they are not. Certain types of boys would never desire to be with certain types of girls as a consequence. Jim preferred Mary because she was judged prettier or more beautiful, and though Charlie would have liked to have had her also, he knew that she would prefer Jim because he was considered better looking than himself; consequently, Charlie and Jane got stuck with each other, whether they wanted it that way or not. But even though this occurred, they were still judging each other according to this physical standard. Before long, they were going out pretty regularly, but something strange began to happen. Jim was falling in love with Mary, even though they never went any further than kissing. He tried on several occasions to feel her up, but she grabbed his hand and slapped his face. Since then, he has stopped, but despite this, he still couldn't wait to be with her and kiss her if she let him. Mary, on the other hand, although she liked him a lot and enjoyed his company, felt that she could get somebody much better, so she kept him on a string while continuing to search for someone closer to her ideal. Charlie, in the meantime, was not attracted to Jane that much since he knew that she had much less to offer than he did, which placed her on the defensive and at a disadvantage because her desire to possess him would always be greater than his desire to possess her, assuming that she had any desire for him at all. Finally, she fell madly in love with him because she began to give him privileges, which resulted in her being screwed every other night. But he didn't want to get married and started to indulge with another girl. Before long, he fell in love with this other individual because she was considered a much more attractive person and because she liked to play all kinds of games that were much more exciting, so he decided to get away from Jane because she was now becoming a nuisance, constantly pestering him to get married or to continue making love. The fact that she was in love with him and that he would hurt her by leaving was never a consideration because he didn't want to spend the rest of his life with someone he was not in love with, so he broke her heart. But now she had developed the habit of making love and liked it so much that she began to look for sexual companions. Soon she was considered a good thing, but still wanting to get married, she went away on a vacation where nobody knew her. She got screwed quite a bit, but nobody fell in love with her. Jim, on the other hand, fell madly in love with Mary because she was considered of much greater value than other girls. In addition to being beautiful, she never gave him what he wanted, and he always desired more than what she gave. Eventually, she broke his heart by leaving him for someone who was uncertain of whether he wanted her because she was judged of lesser value on the scale of physical perfection, and this made her want him all the more. Jim was so hurt by Mary that he played it cool from then on by making girls fall in love with him first; then he could take or leave them without getting hurt. Soon, he had several women in love with him, one of whom committed suicide when she discovered her pregnancy and his engagement to someone else. He eventually married a wealthy girl whose brother was having an affair with Charlie's stepsister's niece, even though her father objected to her running around with a dope addict who was taking too many trips to see God. These trips wouldn't have been so bad, but he never got his pilot's license. I forgot to tell you. Charlie's cousin shacked up with a married woman who had three dope addicts for children, whose father was in an insane asylum because he found her in bed one night with Rin Tin Tin, who bit him so hard in the head for coming in without knocking that he went out of his mind. What are you fellas laughing about? This is a serious business."

"You're a riot, Larry. Well, so what is this supposed to mean?"

"You will understand everything soon enough, but let me review this to make sure you understand what I've been talking about. A perfect example of this difference in looks would be a person considered extremely handsome going out on a blind date (this is perhaps the only way he would go out with her), a girl judged extremely homely. She sees great value in him because, to her, he shows not only tremendous physical but psychological satisfaction as well, since she envisions the compliments and envy of her friends for being able to attract so good-looking an individual. But the only way he would not mind taking her out again, since he sees no other value in her, would be if she were giving him something he liked, as Jane did with Charlie. Consequently, a handsome boy or beautiful girl (remember, however, that these are fallacious words that do not symbolize anything externally real) is bound to have more than their share of admirers, and since it is impossible to marry or satisfy all those in love with them, there are bound to be those who lose and get hurt. These so-called more attractive males and females discover a lack of desire on their own part to possess what they can have for the asking (that is, marriage), which convinces them that they are not in love. In other words, the very moment a girl and boy see that they are admired a little bit more than it is returned, which is occasioned by the projection of a value onto the screen of substance, this other is placed at a disadvantage by being unconsciously or consciously considered inferior in value, and the more this feeling of love is shown, the more they will be uncertain of their love. Unconsciously they feel this other person would be getting a better deal because they know they are closer to this standard of perfection, this ideal, than the other, and so, since it is difficult to desire the possession of what is already possessed, if they want to get married, they keep this other on a string, as I said before, while they search for someone with whom they can fall in love enough to get married, that is, someone who will desire them less in return or consider them inferior to what might be gotten."

"You didn't have to repeat it. I agree with everything you described because I have already experienced it."

"Me too. I pursued my wife for 6 years because she was trying to find her ideal, and in all that time, she never once let me have what I wanted. Finally, when I said either shit or get off the pot, she decided to shit, and it's been a shitty marriage ever since because she felt that she could have married someone closer to her ideal if only I hadn't rushed her. But now that I'm having this affair with Mary (she decided to come back to me after her other relationships failed), I can tolerate this lack of sexual passion in our marriage."

"Is your wife having an affair?"

"I don't think she is, but I really don't care and hope she is. As long as I have Mary, it's a chore I can do without."

"That's what he says, but I don't believe him."

THE SECRET

"This is unimportant anyway. Now, when boys and girls start dating, most of them are too young to accept the responsibilities of marriage, but they still have a normal desire for the opposite sex, which allows them to develop habits of kissing, petting, and fooling around in general. This encourages the one who is judged inferior in value, less pretty or handsome, in other words, the one whose desire is greater, to fall in love. If, in this case, it is the girl and she considers herself good, that is, she adheres to the moral code, she will compel the boy, as much as possible, to commit himself in some way by going steady, becoming engaged, or just confessing his love, before she allows any privileges. But if he does not want to commit himself and she is afraid of losing him, she might try to hold him by giving him more and more and more and more to whet his appetite for still more. Consequently, there were girls who lost the boys they wanted for their husbands by giving them too much (they went all the way — and then some), which made some boys lose their desire to possess what was now theirs without all the responsibility (although there were some who wanted to get married all the more to guarantee the experience); and there were girls who lost out by not giving them enough to whet their appetite. In either case, they were seriously hurt because they were rejected by the person they loved and wanted for their husband. This is why going steady and becoming engaged, unless a couple ends up getting married, could make matters worse because this is no real security, and if the boy should leave after a girl commits herself to the point where she is going the extreme, as Charlie did, any number of things might be preferred as a consequence of this broken heart."

"What about this line of demarcation between a good girl and a bad girl? When I indulged before getting married, I considered such girls cheap and lost all desire to marry any of them. My wife was a good girl; otherwise, I could not have fallen in love with her."

"Let me show you how confused you really are. If the situation were reversed and your wife were chasing you, she might have been willing to become a bad girl, as you expressed it, in the hope that your desire would be aroused enough to marry her. Now, what makes a good girl become bad if not for falling in love with the wrong person, that is, falling for someone who doesn't want her after she has given in to him? And would you have called your wife a bad girl if she had indulged with you before marriage?"

"No, because she was a virgin when I married her."

"In other words, indulging before marriage isn't what makes a girl bad in your eyes, but only when she indulges with more than one person."

"He's a hundred percent right, Charlie. But how is it possible to prevent a girl from indulging with more than one person if she wants to leave the first boy who makes love to her? In other words, how is it possible to prevent them from seeing greater value in someone else? Even if you remove words like beautiful, I would still be drawn to one type of person rather than another. I like Elizabeth Taylor, Lana Turner, and Mary, and I would be attracted in this direction even if there were no words such as beautiful and gorgeous."

THE SECRET

"This much is true, but right now you prefer one girl to another not only because she appeals to you more but also because you know she will appeal to others more. Presently, you could not be attracted to anyone considered ugly or homely because such a choice is judged by the word itself, and you would be criticized for it. But when these words of critical judgment are removed, and they will be soon enough, then your preference cannot be compared to an external ideal of greater value."

"He's right, Charlie. I know if I were never influenced by these words, I would have no way of judging one person more attractive. It's true that I might prefer an aquiline to a straight nose or straight to buck teeth, but I would never be able to judge one person prettier because of my preference without the word. But I think I see a fallacy. Even if this world came about, wouldn't you have the same kind of problem if a girl with straight teeth and a straight nose wanted someone with buck teeth and an aquiline nose? Even if she consented to go out with him, wouldn't she be constantly on the lookout for her ideal?"

"That's a very good point he just made. And if Buck Teeth ended up marrying Straight Teeth because Separated Teeth never came along, isn't it possible for Buck Teeth to have an illicit affair with Separated Teeth — that is, if Separated Teeth also wanted Buck Teeth? And what if Buck Teeth was not the ideal of Separated Teeth, then she could be having one affair while looking for her precious, precious Doll, No Teeth, a guy whose teeth never get in the way. Where's the difference, even if the words like beautiful and ugly are removed?"

"The difference lies in the fact that you have completely forgotten the definition of love. These differences — teeth, noses, and shapes in general — are secondary, not primary factors. The word love, remember, symbolizes a conscious or unconscious desire, in varying degrees, for a sexual relation of some kind, and this is easily proven by the fact that it is impossible for a boy or girl to fall in love with or be physically attracted to someone, no matter how physically appealing this individual might be considered, if they know in advance that this person was born without sexual organs, which knowledge makes them aware that this freak of nature is incapable of giving or receiving sexual satisfaction. In other words, a sexually satisfied girl doesn't care what her man looks like except when she, who is so pretty, is judged for going out with or marrying such a homely person."

"I agree one hundred percent with the definition, but sexual organs are something that everybody takes for granted. Therefore, since each person has his own individual taste, whether it is Buck or Straight Teeth, and if he can't find his ideal — not an ideal that exists externally or is judged better or prettier, but what he likes better — then he would not be completely satisfied if he believes that a sexual relationship with Straight Teeth would be ideal."

"But you have made two assumptions that will be proven false. One, that a boy and girl will not be able to find these secondary factors that appeal to them mutually; and two, that should this be the case, they would still consider these secondary features of importance even after they are completely, one hundred percent sexually satisfied. Removing these words like beautiful and handsome (and we are given no choice), which makes everybody equal in value, would also increase their chances of finding the secondary differences that appeal to them. In this world, one hundred boys selecting among one hundred girls would invariably choose the prettiest, the next prettiest, and so on down the line; and the girls would pick the handsomest, the next in line, and so on, which would present quite a problem since many in this group would have to settle for what they really don't want. But when these standards are removed, this cannot take place, and I will demonstrate that in such a group there exist one hundred perfectly balanced equations of mutual love and devotion, and that not one couple will ever desire to break up or commit adultery. However, before I demonstrate this, let me show you exactly why all these words, such as handsome and beautiful, must come to an end. So, tell me, how is it humanly possible for you to classify people as inferior in value, which is a hurt to them, when you know that they will never blame you for doing this because your will is not free? But you know you don't have to hurt them this way by calling others beautiful, which places them in a category of being ugly, unless you want to, for over this you know you have mathematical control; and when it fully dawns on you that they must excuse what you can never justify, you are compelled to stop using all such words because it is impossible to derive the smallest amount of satisfaction under the changed conditions.

Now, when a boy and girl reach the age of sex in the new world, with the knowledge of what it means that man's will is not free, they know that it is impossible for any person to desire hurting them when it is known in advance that there will be no blame. Consequently, when a girl accepts her first date with a boy who appeals to her and then finds herself falling in love, whether it is returned or not (this is the key to the problem, which must be worked backwards to understand the solution), she is completely unafraid to offer her body because she knows, just as certain as two plus two equals four, that when it fully dawns on the boy that she will never hold him responsible for making her pregnant (nor will anybody alive), for developing a sexual habit only to leave and never return, for making her fall all the more in love with no intention of marrying her (staying with her)... I say, when it fully dawns on him that she will never hold him responsible for this terrible hurt because he knows she must excuse everything he does — although he knows it would be his responsibility since nothing can make him do what he makes up his mind not to do — it becomes mathematically impossible for him to derive any satisfaction whatever from deflowering her under these conditions. Could you, with a clear conscience, take away a girl's virginity when you are absolutely certain that no one, not even the girl to be hurt, will ever blame you for this?"

"I couldn't. I don't know about Charlie."

"I couldn't either, but this still isn't proof of what you said you were going to do."

"I'm not finished yet, either. Now when a boy discovers, through these undeniable relations, that a girl is perfectly willing to go the extreme once he has won her affection or stimulated her desire sufficiently, he recognizes that there is no advantage, in fact a complete waste of time, to pay flattering compliments and hand her a line when knowing that he will be compelled to refuse her body when it is offered... unless he is serious with her. This knowledge completely revolutionizes courtship and dating. Since it is only natural for boys and girls to desire kissing, petting, and fooling around in general, unless restrained by a rigid adherence to the moral code, it doesn't take long before this desire for sexual intercourse is aroused. However, when the boy fully realizes that should he ever get the girl to the point where he won't have a problem getting her to submit, as was just explained, he is compelled to take out only the kind of girl that he doesn't want to hurt, the kind who, when she offers her body on the altar of love, it will never be rejected."

"But supposing she isn't in love enough to want him for her husband? After all, there's a big difference between desiring to have a sexual relationship and selecting a mate for the rest of one's life."

"That's just the point you overlooked, Charlie. There is no difference. Let me show you why. You see, in the new world, when a boy asks a girl for a date, he is actually saying to her, in so many words, 'Honey, you appeal to me very much from every point of view, and I am going to do everything in my power to make love to you if you go out with me. And the girl, if he appeals to her from every point of view, answers him by saying, in so many words, 'Honey, I know what you want, and you can have it.' Knowing that once they start kissing and petting, they would be hurt very much if denied this sexual satisfaction, she is compelled to accept only the kind of date that will appeal enough from the very outset, so she won't have to reject him when his body is offered. She also knows, when accepting this date, that his desire for her will increase only by arousing and satisfying him, and he knows, when asking for this date, that her desire for him will increase for the same reason. Consequently, they are given no choice, and when in a fond embrace his hand begins to wander, instead of checking this motion as a girl was compelled to do to feel clean and decent because this was no indication that he would want her for his wife (if anything, the other way), she only encourages him all the more, as he encourages her. Obviously, both of them will become extremely passionate and desire to go the extreme, but the girl will desire this very much without the slightest fear that the boy will ever hurt her by leaving, and the very moment they indulge, with or without contraception, they sincerely pledge their love and are married until death do they part."

"Why are they married? There was no license or ceremony pronouncing them husband and wife. And how can you possibly know they will desire to stay together for the rest of their lives without committing adultery?"

"How long would it take a car traveling at an average speed of 60 miles an hour to go 93 million miles?"

"Tell him, Charlie."

"Sixty times 24 equals 1440 miles; 1440 miles, which represents one day, will divide into 93 million miles (64,583 days), and 365 days will divide into approximately 176 years."

"But how can you know this when the car won't arrive until 176 years later? Suppose the car broke down, had a few flat tires, and maybe needed another driver or two?"

"We are assuming, that's what you said, that the car travels at an average speed of 60 miles an hour."

"And you are able to do this just by extending mathematical relations. I am going to do the same thing with this married couple. I am going to set up mathematical conditions that will force them, of their own free will, to prefer traveling the full length of their lives together without ever desiring to commit adultery or get a divorce, and they will be given no choice because they will want what they see and will know how to get it."

"But they are definitely not married yet, remember? The fact that they indulged doesn't make them husband and wife. Besides, you could have young kids (possibly fifteen and sixteen) having sexual intercourse. Something just doesn't seem right."

"The only thing that isn't right is your inability to see where you are wrong. If a boy should take a wife without having a job and she becomes pregnant, he would know that her parents would never hold him responsible for throwing this burden on their shoulders; neither would she. Therefore, since the thought of this gives him no satisfaction whatsoever, he prevents it from arising by not marrying at too young an age."

"I wasn't referring so much to pregnancy as sexual intercourse between very young children."

"I see you have a set standard as to when they should get married; is that correct? Just remember one thing, Charlie. By judging the age of nubility, you are blaming them if they get married before you think they should. Since we are not going to blame them anymore for anything, God is plainly telling you to mind your own business. Believe me, he doesn't need you to help him. He created their bodies with a built-in standard as to when it is time to get married, so don't worry about it."

"But suppose a boy and girl desire to get married and can't find a partner?"

"This won't be possible in the new world."

"Or suppose he can't find a job to assume the responsibilities of marriage, but still wants sex? Under these conditions, he and the girl are both hurt, and who is striking the first blow then?"

"Such a situation could never arise, but your question will be answered very shortly when I get to the economic world, so just be patient. As to whether these kids are married, let me ask you this question: Wouldn't it be an insult to man's intelligence to criticize a marriage celebrating half a century of genuine happiness just because this young boy and girl decided to get married without the ceremony and blessing of a rabbi or priest, without an exchange of rings, without a license granted by others? Criticizing such happiness because this couple didn't conform to the prevailing customs — although absolutely necessary under the existing conditions — is equivalent to criticizing a hand of bridge played perfectly because the cards were not cut by the person on the dealer's right, or is it left? In our present world, a couple can get married without having sexual intercourse and can have the latter without the former, but in the new world, soon to unfold, it will be impossible to have one without the other because they are one and the same."

THE SECRET

"I can see certain things very clearly now. By making it impossible for a boy to take away a girl's virginity unless he hurts or marries her, and since he cannot desire to hurt her under the changed conditions, sex becomes a very serious business with only one alternative — marriage. This compels boys and girls to search out, well in advance, the kind of person they want to spend the rest of their lives with, no matter what their preference is."

"But let me point this out, Charlie. The differences that now make a difference will not be present in the new world, and when a boy asks a girl for a date... I mean, asks for her hand in marriage (same difference, because there will be nothing to stop them from going all the way), there will be very little to make her say no. But if he definitely does not appeal to her for any reason, she will simply turn him down, just as a boy will never ask a girl to date him if she doesn't appeal enough for sexual intercourse."

"Couldn't a girl ask a boy?"

"Of course not, because he must assume the responsibility of supporting his wife and children, and she can't make this judgment for him. . ."

"Unless she has enough money."

"In this world, boys and girls never give much thought to the consequences of their actions, and when somebody falls in love and gets hurt, the answer is, 'What am I supposed to do, marry the girl when I'm not in love? She knew what she was doing.' And then her father says, 'You'd better marry her, or I'll kill you.' By being constantly blamed, he was allowed to shift his responsibility, but he had no choice because the pressure for a sexual relationship was striking the first blow.

By removing all the blame, the pressure is also removed; consequently, he is compelled, of his own free will, to assume complete responsibility for everything he does while being denied any satisfaction in hurting her. Under these conditions, which must come about when the principles are understood, there is no possibility for unrequited love to develop, no chance for any girl to be swept off her feet and lose her virginity out of wedlock, no chance to sin, and no opportunity for a boy and girl to hurt each other in any way where sex is concerned because all the factors truly responsible are prevented from arising. The first time they mate, which makes them man and wife since they will never desire to leave each other, as you will soon see, is the holiest of all unions because it is steeped in a feeling of mutual love and respect, a perfectly balanced equation of desire at this moment in their lives."

"Jim, do you realize what he's just accomplished? If it were not for the fact that I see myself losing 40 grand, I would take my hat off to him, but instead, I would like to call the bet off or make some kind of settlement."

"Don't look so down in the dumps, fellas; I haven't won yet. You will soon see how everything ties together, especially when I show you how this married couple will be compelled, of their own free will, to have this balanced equation of sexual desire all through their lives, that is, have a hotter or more passionate relationship than you can ever have presently. However, before I demonstrate this, I am going to perform another miracle by putting a permanent end to all carelessness. Right now, we have more people killed in automobile accidents than you can fully realize. These collisions take place only because man operates on 75% of his potential power, which is insufficient to prevent what nobody wants, even though he is doing everything in his power to prevent it. By understanding what it means that man's will is not free, we plug in the extra 25% and then have the power to prevent what nobody wants. Consequently, all automobile accidents that are the result of carelessness must come to an end, but I would like to observe how related automobile accidents are to what we are faced with, not only in marriage but everywhere. We are having constant collisions of desire, but to balance this equation during our years of development, God was compelled to have good and evil, and the balance was perfect. But now that we have developed sufficiently to see his laws, which reveal him, he snips off the evil and attaches good so that the balance still remains perfect. To understand the magnitude of this mathematical problem, which requires for its solution that there be no collisions of desire anywhere in the world, I shall offer you a problem as a comparison."

"Is this the one I'm thinking of, the one I couldn't even understand the question, and Charlie never answered?"

"No, it is not, but it is related to collisions, so to speak. A teacher has 15 students whom she takes on a walk 7 days a week, but since she believes in order and variety of company on these daily strolls through the woods, she decides to arrange them in groups of three in a column formation. But every day, for seven days, each student is never twice with the same student in a group, which means that if A has already been with B and C, he can walk with D on the next day, but since D has already been with E and F, they must select together one of the remaining students from G to O. When you realize that these 15 students must all be arranged this way for 7 days, you can see that it is not a simple problem, unless you see the relations. Now just compare these 15 kids whose desires do not conflict on these walks (there is no collision) with the billions of people in the world whom God is going to direct, so there will never be any collisions of desire."

"What's the answer?"

"You saw part of the answer in premarital relations..."

"I mean the answer to that other problem."

"That's your problem, not mine. If you want to waste your time with it, that's your business. I want to get back to my work."

CHAPTER SIX
CARELESSNESS

"Now carelessness, just as the word implies, is an 'I do not care' attitude. It arises from several factors. There are young boys and girls who want to make an impression on their friends, and this requires that they demonstrate their ability to handle a car like a racing driver, but they never give much thought to the other person because man's first concern has always been for himself. If he is willing to risk his own life and happens to take others with him, that's their tough luck. For this reason, you would often hear, 'Drive carefully; the life you save might be your own.' The drunks, dope addicts, and people in a hurry can't stand being behind a slow-moving vehicle, even if this means passing it on a curve or hill. They either don't fully realize the danger or don't care, since the risk is primarily to themselves. Or the showoff wants to give his friends a thrill and demonstrate how to do what really takes guts.

Then there are those who do not care because this requires great effort. Applying brakes when the light changes yellow as an alternative to speeding up and making it so stopping isn't necessary is considered a nuisance, so many times they go through on the red and crash into the driver who starts off before the light has changed to green.

Then there is the mother who is so fed up with the struggle to take care of too many kids, now that she is not in love with her husband anymore, she just doesn't care. She leaves matches and other potentially dangerous items lying around, and when the house catches on fire or they get hurt in some other way, she always comes up with an excuse. But what has added to her carelessness is the fact that she never understood the meaning of fatalism. It is undeniably true that everything happens according to laws over which we have no control, but before something occurs, it is our nature to choose the alternative considered better for ourselves. Consequently, when this belief in fatalism was told to me by a mother who didn't seem to take much care in watching her children, I asked her, 'If you saw your baby getting ready to crawl in front of a truck, would you pick him up or let him go?' 'Naturally, I would grab him.' 'Why, if you believe in fate?' 'I can see that danger,' she replied. 'In other words,' I said, 'once you have done everything in your power to prevent an accident, and then it occurs, you can say it was fate.'

Carelessness has allowed airplanes to crash into each other or explode because the mechanics failed in their duty. It has allowed ships to ram each other, hotels, nightclubs, houses, etc., to burst into flames. It has allowed tires to blow out and brakes to fail; even buildings to collapse. There is no telling how many lives have been lost or mutilated (blinded, crippled, or what have you), all because of carelessness. And liability insurance came into existence out of absolute necessity to help prevent the aftereffects of an accident; otherwise, we would have more killing.

"I don't know about you guys, but if it had not been for my ability to drive defensively, I would have been killed or hospitalized at least a dozen times."

"I agree that defensive driving is extremely important... in this world, that is. I don't know about the new world."

"Everybody doesn't have the coordination and skill to drive defensively, just as they do not have other talents and skills. However, everybody does have the ability to learn and apply the don'ts of good driving. Now observe how God compels this to come about.

When an accident occurs in our present environment, the people involved are standing on this spot called <u>here,</u> and are preparing to move to the next spot called <u>there</u>. They are more dissatisfied than usual because their car has just been wrecked, although nobody was hurt, so what do they do for satisfaction? If there were no witnesses, they hurl accusations at each other until the police arrive. The person who did not have the right of way could possibly, in a courtroom with a clever lawyer, make the innocent party appear guilty to determine which insurance company will be held liable. If the one who had the right of way was under the influence of liquor, even though the accident was not his fault, he is already judged guilty, as this offers a perfect excuse. But when an extremely serious accident occurs where, let us say, two children and their mother were instantly killed, while the father and the other driver were thrown clear, to assume responsibility for this is too horrible to bear, which compels them to think up a million and one excuses as to why it was the other person's fault. If there were witnesses and both drivers knew it was not the father's responsibility, the guilty party would welcome whatever punishment could be dished out so that he could pay dearly for what he did, and the liability insurance he carries just in case helps him in a small way to pay part of the price. If it were the father's fault, he might not be able to stand this terrible feeling of guilt and might be forced to find some reason as to why this accident was unavoidable; otherwise, he could kill himself. However, to make it possible for him to continue living, the law will charge him with manslaughter, and he will have to serve a prison sentence, which he welcomes because this also helps pay for what he did. How many times will the ability to use just these words, true or false, make someone feel so much better? 'I couldn't help myself. It was not my fault. It was unavoidable.' And how many times in the course of history have the innocent been compelled to pay the price of the guilty, just because man was able to shift his responsibility? But watch what happens when we apply our basic principle. Remember, however, the new world is not yet here, so we are going to imagine the same accident that will not occur, just so we can see why it will not.

The two survivors pick themselves up off the ground, and both know that no one will be coming along to blame them for this horrible tragedy. The police are not going to smell their breath or give them other tests because there are no more police. The father is weeping bitterly over the loss of his family (this could be the result of any kind of carelessness). People standing around are shocked at the sight. An ambulance arrives to carry off the dead, and tow trucks arrive to clean up the debris. Now let us imagine that the driver of the other car knows it was his fault, but he also knows that the father will never blame him for what was done because everyone alive must excuse what he did, since it is now known that his will is not free, which means that he couldn't help himself. But he knows, before something happens, that he doesn't have to do what causes accidents through carelessness, unless he wants to, for over this he has mathematical control, and when this fully dawns on him, and when he is prevented from saying, 'I couldn't help myself.' 'It was not my fault.' 'It was unavoidable' — because no one is blaming him — he will be unable to find any satisfaction whatever and will be compelled to live out his life with this horrible feeling of guilt, having no way to ever get rid of it. He would like to be blamed, criticized, condemned, punished, beaten up by the father, and hated, but he knows these things will never take place because nobody alive holds him responsible. He would like to write a check to compensate for what he did, but nobody is suing or blaming him in any way, which compels him to hold himself responsible."

"But supposing it really was the father's fault?"

"Well, is anybody blaming the driver of the other car? So how would it be possible for him to say, 'It was not my fault but his?' No matter how unbearable it was for him to feel this responsibility, just imagine how the father must feel to know that he was, or might have been, responsible for the deaths of his children, although this difference could hardly pass through the eye of a needle."

"Why did you say, 'might have been?'"

"In other words, if the father was a little uncertain of what actually happened, as long as he knows it might have been his fault, he will suffer just as much as if he were certain, because there is no way he can find out when no one blames him."

"I'm beginning to see the effect of this even in smaller accidents, because the person who caused it is made to realize how much inconvenience and trouble he puts people through who refuse to blame him in any way for doing what he knows they must excuse, and he, for the very first time, cannot justify."

"Once all mankind are taught what it means that man's will is not free, they are permitted to see, well in advance, a situation that is too horrible to contemplate; consequently, the only avenue open for needed satisfaction is to prevent it from arising because there is no way they can do anything afterwards — under the changed conditions. This means that whatever the other driver did that caused the accident would be listed among the don'ts of good driving, and he would never desire to go against these. People who are in a hurry to beat a traffic signal will do just the opposite: never try to beat it and never be in a position where they are compelled to go through a red light or screech their brakes. If, however, there is no traffic coming and the light is red, there is no reason to stay because its purpose is to stop the other traffic so they can go. There will be no need for speed limits because nobody will desire to travel at a speed that endangers others. If someone wishes to go out to a strip and race at two hundred miles an hour, this is his business, just so there is no possibility of someone getting hurt, other than himself; and if there are others that wish to race against him, this is their business, just so there are no drivers in this race that don't want to be.

Right now, we need a license to drive, and before this is granted, we are given certain tests to see if we qualify, which means that part of our responsibility has already been shifted. In other words, people who are really not qualified to sit behind a wheel are made to think they are by receiving permission, and should someone make the comment, 'You shouldn't be allowed to drive a car,' the response would be, 'The government thinks so, or I would not have been given a license.' But in the new world, there will be no such thing as a license to drive, and the only person to tell you that you are sufficiently trained and ready will be you yourself. Even the teachers in driving schools will never tell you because there is no need for them to assume responsibility. They will have a thorough course of training, which will include all the causes of accidents through carelessness, and you will know whether you are ready by comparing your ability with the tough driving standards set by the driving schools. Today we say, 'Obey the laws or else you will be punished.' Tomorrow we say, 'Don't obey the laws of good driving if you don't want to, but if someone gets hurt as a consequence, it will be mathematically impossible to blame anybody but yourself.'"

"Although I agree with everything you have demonstrated thus far, reluctantly, and think it is absolutely marvelous, I still can't see how it will be possible to prevent adultery and divorce."

"Remember, just because you can't see the possibility of something does not make it impossible. But you are in for quite a surprise."

"Although I wouldn't bet a nickel more against you, Larry, and would like to get out of this bet if at all possible, I agree with Charlie that it does seem impossible in spite of what you just accomplished. I can't see how you can satisfy the whole human race, and that's what you must do with your equation, which includes communism as well as capitalism."

"You keep forgetting one thing. I am not the one who will solve this problem. The astronomer who first observed the invariable laws between the planets, moon, and sun didn't cause the eclipse; he perceived certain relations that made him aware it would occur at a certain time. And just because I have observed the invariable laws inherent in the mankind system, which allowed me to see the end of all war and crime because of what it means that man's will is not free, doesn't mean that I am causing this to come about. The most I can do is reveal God's laws, which give us no choice but to move in a certain direction for satisfaction, because we are a part of his laws. You will see how effective these laws are tomorrow, aside from what I have already demonstrated, when I put a permanent end to all adultery and divorce."

CHAPTER SEVEN
MARRIAGE

"Would you believe it? I couldn't wait for this morning! I stayed awake half the night trying to find a flaw, but there isn't any I could see. Do you realize what this guy has accomplished? Is it any wonder my Ph.D. degree couldn't be of any use here? Have you fully grasped this: Man does not have five senses, and his will is not free? This is incredible, absolutely fantastic! Of course, the most difficult of all the problems is yet to come, putting a permanent end to war and crime... but that magic elixir is too much. I wish I could be happy over all this, but 40 grand is a lot of money for this kind of entertainment. I have a feeling we lost our dough."

"Are you telling me. I still haven't told my wife. I stayed awake half the night, too, trying to figure out how to tell her about this bet I made, but I can't get up enough nerve. She just might shoot me. I also think we lost our money. Talk him into some kind of settlement. Here he comes now."

"Hi fellas! Are you ready to continue where we left off?"

"If we give you a thousand dollars each, would you call the bet off?"

"I'll do better than that. I'll call it off, and you can keep your money."

"You're kidding! You can't be telling the truth! I must be hearing things! Charlie, did you hear what I heard, or is this another aspect of that magic elixir?"

"I'm not joking. This was the only way I could get somebody to listen to what I had discovered. I knew there was no way you could win when I made the bet, simply because two plus two equals four. I intended to do exactly what I'm now doing the moment you saw there was no way you could win."

"I can't thank you enough, Lar. You just lifted a heavy weight off my shoulders."

"I still can't believe it! Your friend is a prince. There is one way I'm going to thank you. Nothing under the sun could make me not want to listen to everything you have to say. So continue."

"Before you begin, one thing puzzled me quite a bit last night, not regarding what you already demonstrated... that I found to be flawless, but regarding marriage. How is it possible to have a balanced equation of sexual desire when the male plays an active, the female a passive role? If for any reason he can't get a hard-on, she's in trouble. Charlie hasn't experienced this yet, but do you know how many times I've been compelled to use my finger to make my wife come? But what can I do when it won't stand up or collapses like an accordion at the wrong time? With Mary, it's quite different. I get so hot that my penis is like a phallic symbol, and I enjoy kissing every part of her body. But I realize that this desire is the result of passion. She loves to blow me, and I love to reciprocate, but the thought of doing this to my wife sickens me. And to show you how innocent she is, one time I said in a joke, 'How about giving me a blow job?' and she thought I meant for her to blow on it. This is the problem I cannot see you solving because I know that even if I married Mary and lived with her for the same number of years, it would be the same exact situation as in my previous marriage. I said it before, and I'll say it again; it seems an impossible situation to correct... but I wouldn't bet on it. Well, what's the answer?"

"In order to solve the problem of marriage and prevent the consideration of adultery and divorce from ever arising, a perfectly balanced equation of sexual desire must always prevail, from beginning to end. How this is accomplished is something marvelous to behold, and if my will were free, I would take credit for it. So put on your thinking caps and follow me carefully.

Now it is extremely important to understand that when a boy and girl, in the new world, consummate their feelings with a complete sexual relationship that results in an orgasm, they are going to fall desperately in love and desire each other all the more because this exciting thrill of physical contact is a new experience that has become associated with one particular person to whom they must turn for satisfaction. Soon, each will be absolutely dependent on the other for what the body now craves, and if this were stopped, as frequently happened in the world of free will for various reasons that occasioned serious consequences, it would be the worst form of torment. Yet there are two individual desires involved, and it is impossible, in the new world, for one person to desire obligating the other, not only because this is a form of advance blame (this was not yet explained), which is a judgment of what is right for someone else, but mainly because it could not be preferred when it is realized that this would not be conducive to a harmonious relationship. However, this radiant wife, who has been falling more and more in love with her husband as they continue making passionate love, as they continue to look forward to the warmth and ecstasy of this sexual satisfaction, knows positively that it is absolutely impossible for her husband to ever desire another sexual partner — despite the fact that she knows he is not under any obligation to remain and completely free to do anything he wants — just as long as he knows she is definitely in love with him, because she knows that he knows if he left her under these conditions this would break her heart for which he would never be blamed, as this desire to hurt her so deeply must be considered by others as God's will or a compulsion over which he has no control. But he knows it is not God's will or a compulsion over which he has no control, because he also knows that he doesn't have to break her heart unless he wants to. Therefore, this great security is assured to the wife just as long as she shows her husband that she truly loves him, for then only can his leaving her for another sexual companion be a source of hurt."

"But supposing a wife stops showing her husband that she loves him?"

"We have just arrived at the other half of the equation. This young husband, so much in love with his wife at this moment in his life, knows also that she will never desire to leave him just as long as she knows he is in love with her. Consequently, since he knows that her desire to leave depends solely on him being out of love with her, which separation would break his own heart, for which she cannot be blamed since he can prevent it, he is compelled, for his own security and happiness, to prefer doing everything in his power to completely satisfy his wife to show that he is not out of love with her so that this desire to stop showing her husband that she loves him will never arise in her. Knowing that his own security with the person he loves depends on her love, which he can control by showing his own, and knowing that her own security with the person she loves depends on his love, which she can control by showing her own, they are given no choice but to do everything in their power for each other, as that alternative considered better for themselves because it is the only means by which they can prevent what they do not want. Therefore, when it is understood that sexual satisfaction is the true meaning of love and when it decreases in a nonmutual manner, a marriage deteriorates, it is obvious that the surest way to success in conjugal affairs is to arouse the sexual passion of the other since this demonstrates, in an undeniable manner, that you want your partner to be in love with you, which reveals that you don't want another mate since the love of your wife makes this a mathematical impossibility.

By the same reasoning, as your wife makes efforts to arouse your desire, she reveals that she wants your love, which makes you conscious that she does not want another husband or lover, since your love for her makes this also a mathematical impossibility. Consequently, when a husband

and wife realize from the very beginning that the security of their extreme happiness depends on arousing and satisfying the sexual passion of the other — without imposing one ounce of obligation because this is advance blame — they are given no choice as to what is better since any word or action that decreases the desire to have a passionate relationship only reveals a lack of love by tacitly blaming the sexual desire of the other."

"You are too much! I can see that this is completely mathematical, except for two things that still have to be demonstrated. How is it possible to have a marriage without any obligation, and what is required to show one's love?"

"Maybe it did to you, Charlie, but what he just demonstrated made no sense to me. You have taken for granted that sexual passion can be aroused after many years of wedlock, and I say it can't be."

"Do you want to bet your 50 grand again?"

"Not a chance of it. I didn't mean to say, 'it can't be done,' only that I think it can't be. Will answering Charlie's questions clarify everything?"

"Yes, it will, and you will find it very simple to understand. Every couple will be compelled to remove from their relationship every bit of advance blame. This means that Judgment Day has arrived at last, the time when all mankind will be compelled to stop judging what is right for others and judge only themselves. How this comes about with the aid of our basic principle, Thou Shall Not Blame, is also marvelous to behold, but let me explain exactly what I mean.

THE SECRET

In order for a person to blame others, he must feel that he has been hurt or wronged, which justifies some form of retaliation. But when he judges in advance for them, he makes his judgment a standard for what is right, and when they fail to do what he thinks they should, he blames them. You see, in every human relationship, there are two desires involved, his and theirs, but if to satisfy him, he needs them, then their desire must be taken into consideration, and if they do not want to do what he wants done, then there is nothing he can do about it once the basic principle is introduced. Before that, however, he did something to hurt them for not satisfying his desire. But when he knows he is definitely in the wrong by judging what is right for them, and when it becomes impossible for him to hurt them for not doing what he thinks they should, because he knows they will never blame him, he can find no satisfaction in trying to impose his will. But this imposition was necessary in our present world because they were hurting him with their judgment of what is right. However, when our magic elixir demonstrates mathematically who is wrong where human relations are concerned, then he is given no choice but to change. To understand exactly what I'm talking about, it is necessary to elaborate on the various forms of advance blame — this judging of what is right for someone else — which is wrong. So let me begin by directing my next question to Charlie.

Should you and Alice get married, has it been decided whether you will have twin beds or a double bed?"

"We already talked it over, and both of us agreed to get a double bed. She likes to snuggle, and so do I."

"What would you say if I told you that God is not going to give either of you a choice in this matter, and that you will be compelled, of your own free will, to have two beds always available?"

"Is this because sleeping together decreases passion over time?"

"Sleeping together night after night does decrease passion, but it is not the reason you will have two beds, twin or otherwise. Now tell me, who suggested getting the double bed, you or Alice?"

"She brought it up, and I agreed to it."

"The person who brings it up is the one who strikes this first blow of marriage. Let me show you why. Supposing one night you feel like sleeping alone, wouldn't she be saying to you in so many words, if no other bed was available, 'I want you next to me. Come back here, Charlie.'"

"Yes, she would be saying that, when you come to think of it."

"Which means that in order for Alice to satisfy her desire, which is to sleep with you, she insists that you sacrifice your desire to sleep alone."

"But when I sleep alone, am I not insisting that she sacrifice her desire to sleep with me?"

"Of course not, because your desire to sleep alone makes absolutely no demands on her whatsoever, whereas her desire to sleep with you, should you want to get up, grabs you by the arm and pulls you back. Her desire is selfish because, in order to satisfy it, she insists that you do something for her without considering your desire not to do it. In other words, anytime a husband or wife tells the other what to do, this is a judgment of what is right for someone else, and therefore it is wrong because the person telling the other is blaming in advance the desire not to do it. If you told your son to run downstairs and get you the evening paper, what would you say to him if he replied, 'Go get it yourself?'"

"He knows better than to say that to me."

"Which proves conclusively that by telling him what to do, you are blaming him in advance for not doing it; otherwise, you wouldn't say a word if he refused. How many times has your wife told you to do this or that, and what happens when you give her an excuse?"

"Sometimes she accepts it, but if I just say that I don't feel like doing it, an argument arises."

"Do you understand that in the new world, neither husband nor wife will ever tell the other what to do because this is a form of advance blame, just like the double bed with no other bed available? I want to make sure before I continue."

"I can see the relation, and I agree. So does Charlie, I'm sure."

"Now the next form of advance blame is asking favors, which is a euphemistic way of telling someone what to do. Instead of telling your son to bring you the paper because this is an expression of authority that children often rebel against, let us imagine that you ask him, 'Jimmy, would you mind bringing Dad the paper?' 'I'm too busy.' 'Look here, boy; it's lying right on the sofa; now you bring it up right away.' Stop and think about this very carefully.

'Jim, can you lend me five dollars until Friday?' 'I can't spare it.' 'Don't tell me that. I know you could if you wanted to. Didn't I lend you five, two years ago? Can't you return the favor?' In other words, asking favors blames in advance the possibility of being disappointed, and when you are, you blame. Proof that this is the case is the fact that you could never ask a favor if you knew positively that it would be refused. Therefore, the person who asks favors is in the wrong."

"I definitely see a fallacy; that is, I think I see one. Being aware of what advance blame is could never, in a million years, make people stop telling others what to do, or stop them from asking favors, because there is a definite advantage in being able to get others to run errands for you or be your slave. There's a guy in town... you know him, Lar... Big Buck. I heard him ask someone in a bar to lend him ten dollars, but this guy wouldn't do it. He hit this guy so hard with his fist that he was out for ten minutes. Big Buck then went through his pockets, took out the ten, and then said, 'When I ask you the next time to do me a favor, you'd better think twice before you turn me down.' This guy has twenty people running errands for him because they are scared to death, and there is no difference between this and the authority husbands and wives exercise over each other and their children. The kids are afraid to disobey, and your advance blame will be ignored because man must move in the direction of greater satisfaction, and it is much more satisfying to get people to do your bidding than work yourself, especially when you don't have to pay them anything. And what about the guy who wants to borrow ten dollars from his boss until payday? Is he going to say to himself, 'I can't ask my boss for this because it is a form of advance blame?"

"In the world of free will, Big Buck blames the guy he socked for hurting him by not lending the money. But in the new world, he will know that he is wrong. However, if he still feels like socking this person, that will be his privilege, but he will know well in advance that no one alive, including the person to be hurt, will ever blame him or desire to hurt him in return. By introducing the principle at this point, all bullies, including parents (I shall discuss children separately), will be compelled to lose their desire to bully. This advance blame determines mathematically who is right, and then prevents the desire to do what is wrong.

Another form of advance blame related to asking favors is asking questions. By asking a question, you are actually asking someone to do you a favor. Let me show you that it is the exact same principle as with the double bed. Suppose you asked me, 'Larry, do you know what time it is?'... and I ignored your question. Wouldn't you repeat it? And then if I ignored it the second time, wouldn't you say, 'Have you lost your hearing? I just asked you what the time is.' And each time I refused to answer, wouldn't you get angrier at me? The answer, however, is very simple. By asking me a question, you have blamed me in advance for not answering it, and when I don't, you blame. You have expressed your desire, which is to have me do a favor and answer your question, and you have also judged what my desire should be, which is to satisfy your desire. But you failed to take into consideration the possibility that I might not want to move in that direction, which is my business. Now, because man has never known who is right and wrong in these matters, and because he didn't really care as long as he could threaten some form of hurt to get his way, he was allowed to develop just as he did. But when he knows absolutely and positively that others will never strike back or blame him in any way, no matter what he does to them for not answering his questions or doing his favor, and because he also knows that he is in the wrong, there is only one thing left to do. Stop asking the kind of questions and favors that he can answer and do for himself. If a family had one double bed because they couldn't afford another (impossible in the new world), and the wife decided to get up to sleep by herself on the sofa in the living room, her husband would never say, 'Where are you going?' because he knows she wouldn't even answer this question since it is none of his business. Maybe she is going to the bathroom, to get a glass of water, or to sleep on the sofa. But whatever she decides to get up for after making love, this is her business, or his business if he is the one. However, if they want to tell the other where they are going, this is their business. Since they know what is right and wrong at last, they are compelled to mind their own business, but this is not a criticism of those today who have been minding other people's business, because they were compelled by God to do everything they did."

"What kind of world are we coming to if we can't ask favors or questions anymore? I don't like it."

"Now, Jim, you have to be kidding that you didn't follow me. Nobody is going to tell you not to ask questions or favors or tell others what to do, for this will be your business if you desire to continue that way under the changed conditions.

THE SECRET

All this is doing is forcing people, of their own free will or desire, to become extremely intelligent by doing everything for themselves without expecting others to. You could have gone into the kitchen, where a clock is on the wall, to find out the time, but you moved in the direction of least resistance, which was natural in this environment. But when you can't impose your will on others anymore — because to do so, you must strike the first blow of hurt for which you will never be blamed — you are compelled to think like never before to save yourself all unnecessary work. Since you can't order your wife to get you the paper, you will make sure you take it up with you when you go the first time, and when you go downstairs, you will make absolutely sure you have everything needed because you won't be able to send her back up, or she you. However, something fantastic takes place as a consequence. Knowing that they will never be asking favors of each other, they will desire to do everything in their power to make each other happy, and they start to think in this direction like never before. She prepares him a glass of ice-cold lemonade because she knows he likes it, and when she hands it to him, he is extremely pleased and says, 'Thanks, Honey.'"

"Doesn't she say, 'You're welcome?'"

"She could, but she doesn't, simply because he knows this; otherwise, she wouldn't have done it. He is not expecting any response."

"Is she expecting him to thank her? And if she is, isn't this a judgment of what is right for him? In other words, isn't this advance blame when he fails to do what she thinks he should?"

"You are perfectly right, but she is not expecting any thanks or payment for what she did, and that is why he appreciates what she did all the more. But though this is not the way it was in the old world, please remember that it had to be; otherwise, you will criticize and laugh at those who were that way before the transition gets officially launched. You will understand all this much better when it is reviewed the second and even the third time."

"But this doesn't rule out asking questions and favors altogether, does it?"

"Of course not. When someone falls overboard and yells, 'Help! Help! Help!', he is asking you to do him a favor and save his life, and you will desire to because he cannot do this for himself; therefore, the only favors and questions that will ever be asked will be those we cannot do and answer for ourselves."

"But when a husband and wife are in the mood to make love, this is something neither one can do for themselves, and wouldn't they be yelling, 'Help! Help! Help! Please satisfy me sexually because I'm in the mood to make love,' which is a judgment of what is right for the other and a form of obligation?"

"But you are not absolutely certain, are you, Jim?"

"Not enough to bet my money. It just seems impossible for this desire to be so mutual that they will fall into each other's arms at the exact same time; otherwise, there must be this obligation."

"I know how it sounds and how it looks, but sounds and looks are deceiving. Let me prove this by continuing to follow our mathematical standard and slide rule: Thou Shall Not Blame.

Now, the reason you cannot tell your partner you are in the mood is that you know she loves you and would be willing to do anything to show her love, but this would only reveal your selfishness. You cannot touch her because this only expresses your desire, while her desire may be that you leave her alone. Consequently, you have only one thing left to do. You must arouse her desire, or she yours, without touching her, using any method you prefer; that is, you can dress or undress, use what words you want, use what aphrodisiacs you like — do anything that you feel will arouse her to accept your invitation. Remember, however, you have a pretty good indicator, so does she, and when both of you read the temperature on each other's indicator, an invitation will be accepted by making physical contact with the one who is inviting the other."

"But that's still the same thing. If he extends her an invitation by doing all these things, he is plainly saying, 'I'm in the mood. Please come over here to me since I can't go to you.'"

"This is where your fallacy lies because they are not saying this. In our present world, they would say that, but remember, their security lies in showing their love, which means that they want to do everything in their power for each other. Therefore, when an invitation is extended, this is what they are actually saying: 'Honey, I am very much in the mood to make love to you,' not 'I am in the mood to have you make love to me.' Consequently, when she makes physical contact by accepting his invitation, or vice versa, he is much more interested in satisfying her, one way or another, than himself, while she is more interested in satisfying him."

"He's right, Jim. These are absolutely infallible, undeniable principles. Are there any rules and regulations as to what they can do to each other? After all, there is such a thing as a perverted act."

"You should know better than that by now. This word, like the others, becomes obsolete because there is no such thing, and it is a form of criticism, which is a hurt. They will do to each other whatever they want to do, and this is God's will."

"Supposing I want her to suck my dick?"

"This is her business, not yours. If she wants to do it, then it becomes her business, unless you don't want her to do it. But remember, she wants to satisfy you; she wants to arouse your passion to such a degree that when you climax, you will think you're in heaven, and you will do the same for her."

"But once I come, my passion will be automatically lowered."

"She knows that, and you know that. Therefore, if she is capable of having an orgasm three, four, five or more times, it will be your greatest pleasure to satisfy her any way you can and reserve your capabilities so that your climax, if it is only one, will coincide with her final climax. But don't judge what your capabilities will be in the new world when all arguments are completely removed from your marriage."

"I won't be there, so I don't give a shit. And I still believe we only live once, regardless of what you implied."

THE SECRET

"You'll be there, believe me, and so will everybody else who understands the mathematical relations that reveal this. This will..."

"Supposing they don't understand, does this mean they won't be allowed to enter this Kingdom of God?"

"This is just a figure of speech. Everybody will be there. And this knowledge will arouse your desire to build this new world all the more, because you will know it is being constructed not for your posterity but for yourself. But I'm not ready to reveal this yet."

"I still can't see how all arguments will be prevented from arising when there are so many things they could argue about. For example, suppose I should decide to go to the poolroom after work instead of home for dinner?"

"There is nothing wrong with desiring to play pool, and your wife would never object. But because you want to satisfy her sexually at all times before doing anything else, you will desire to go home to extend her an invitation to see if she is in the mood to have you make love to her, while she will be waiting for you to come home so she can extend an invitation so that she can make love to you. If she isn't, then there would be nothing to stop you from shooting pool, and it would make her happy to see you satisfy your desires just as it would make you happy to see her satisfy hers. But remember, what will arouse your passion will not be the thought of what she will do to you, but what you will do to her. Consequently, you will be impatient all day long to get home to let her read the temperature on your indicator, while she will be dreaming all day of what she would like to do to you, and when you walk through the door you might see her dressed in her sexy negligee, compelling you to accept the invitation immediately."

"But aren't there certain standards of what is right and wrong regarding other things, like raising children, taking care of a house, working, the time each one can spend satisfying other desires, such as bowling, pool, golf, tennis, bridge, chess, etc.? And what about the selection of furniture for their new home or apartment, preparing meals, washing clothes? There has to be a standard of right and wrong."

"There is. The husband's job is to take care of everything that is his business, and her job is to take care of everything that is her business. The selection of the bed he will sleep in is his business, just as making it up or not is also his business. Keeping his clothes clean or dirty, washing the dishes he messes up after eating or leaving them alone, taking out the garbage and trash he accumulates, or not taking this out, will also be his business. Her business will be most of the same things, plus taking care of the children, preparing meals, and taking care of what in the house is not his responsibility, such as how the furniture should be arranged and keeping the rest of the house clean if she wants to."

"I am confused on two points."

"I like the way Charlie expresses himself now. He does not say, 'I see a fallacy,' because he knows there aren't any, and he knows that his education means absolutely nothing right now unless he is using it in some way to earn a living. Oh... but are you in for a surprise when I get to the new economic world. Russia, the United States, and all the nations of the world will love it because, for the first time in history, there will be brotherly love at last and no more wars. Wouldn't that be wonderful?"

"It certainly would, but I'm still confused on those same two points. If there are children, wouldn't it be possible for a husband to take advantage and leave his wife after dinner to play pool all evening and night after night? And why is it her responsibility to arrange the furniture instead of his, or why can't they both be involved? It would be perfectly fair if she would like a chair in one location and he in another to flip a coin. But let's go a step farther. Suppose he is an interior decorator. Shouldn't his knowledge of these things be put to use?"

"In the new world, there will be no interior decorators because nobody will ever desire to spend their money in that direction. Remember, this is your money, and how you spend it is your business. But to answer your question, I shall show you why these decorators and fashion designers must be permanently displaced.

When people visit your home in this world, here is what they say: 'How beautiful! How simply gorgeous! But I don't like where you have that chair. It really doesn't belong by the steps, and that picture should be moved to the other room. But your colors blend beautifully. Who did your decorating?' Now watch what happens in this world when these words are removed from our vocabulary and the basic principle is introduced. The visitor can't say, 'How beautiful! How simply gorgeous!' The only thing she can say is, 'I really and truly love the way you arranged your house,' simply because any criticism is a hurt for which she knows there will be no blame. And since she knows that her hosts also know that she can only pay a compliment, there is no need to say it. It only becomes a value when it is possible to criticize. Consequently, she is compelled to say nothing complimentary or critical, and because everybody in the new world will know this, the husband doesn't care how she arranges the house just so he can place his chair, his lamp, his desk, his bed where he wants his things."

"But supposing they desire the same location?"

"This isn't very likely, although it could happen that they both might desire a different television show at the same time, with only one set available. Then they are compelled to flip a coin, but not for the purpose that it would be done in this world. She would let him watch his show if she won the toss and would visit a friend if it meant that much to her, and she would let him place his things where he wants or she wants, whatever the case may be."

"I understand this point and cannot disagree in any way. But what about the time element, and what about doing things together other than making love?"

"If they don't have money for a babysitter, they will divide the time, after he gets home from work, in a perfectly equal manner. They will take turns staying in with the baby so the other can get out and do whatever is desired. If she feels like seeing a particular movie on her night out, she may extend him an invitation like this several days before: 'Honey, on Friday I'm going to see Gone with the Wind. Would you like to go with me?' Now it is his move. If he says 'yes,' they will plan to hire a babysitter. If he says 'no,' this is his business, and she would never complain. By the same reasoning, if on his night he plans to shoot pool, he could say to her, if he wants to: 'Honey, I'm going to shoot pool tonight; would you care to come along and watch or play a game yourself?' Now it's her move. If she doesn't like pool, this is her business, and she is under no obligation to go."

"I get the whole picture and I think it's just wonderful, great, beautiful! But suppose he decides on her night out to hire a babysitter so he can get out even though it isn't his night; wouldn't this be taking advantage?"

"If they have enough extra money to go out for fourteen nights in a row, the husband, who will be the breadwinner in the majority of cases, would desire very strongly to see that his wife satisfies all her desires to the fullest; consequently, he is prevented from taking advantage of her because this would not be an advantage under the changed conditions, which forces him, of his own free will or desire, to divide this babysitting money in an equal manner, so much for her and so much for him. Then, should he decide to play pool on the night she goes to see Gone with the Wind, she may prefer playing pool on the night he goes to see The Hustler. But under the changed conditions, it is mathematically impossible for an argument to ever arise, which will keep them constantly in the mood to extend each other an invitation to make love."

"Charlie might not be confused anymore, but I am, on one particular point. I understand that it is the wife's responsibility to prepare the meals, as it is his to earn a living. But she could get a job if she wanted to and pay for the babysitter out of her own money, right?"

"Certainly, this is her business, but they will combine their money as one, right down the middle, because any other way would not give them satisfaction since this would be taking advantage, and there can be no advantage when this involves a hurt for which there would never be any criticism."

"I understand this, and I realize that she will want to prepare the best possible meals to satisfy him, but supposing she doesn't like the same food he does?"

"Is anyone compelling her to eat what she doesn't like? She could make what she likes for herself. But because this involves extra work, she will quickly learn to enjoy the same things he likes, unless she doesn't mind the extra work. In this world, the wife prepares what she likes, and when her husband complains, she gives him excuses. By the same reasoning, when he loses money that he needs for necessities and she complains, he gives her excuses. But this will be precluded in the new world by making him realize that should he hurt his family this way, they would never blame him, compelling him to gamble only with the money he can afford to lose. But since he is very anxious to show his love and knows this would not show it, he is also controlled in this way. The basic principle is always there to remind him as to what is right and wrong."

"Supposing, as in Alice's husband's case, a man should get fat and sloppy. He couldn't arouse her no matter how he dressed or undressed or what he said and smelled like."

"If people allow themselves to get out of shape, that is, out of the shape they were in when they got married, then they are blaming in advance the sexual desire of the other; therefore, they are compelled to retain the same figure or physique, if possible, all through life, but only because this would be a hurt to themselves should they not. Remember, he wants to satisfy her, and to do this, he must arouse her to accept his invitation. If he makes himself unappealing to her, he will be denied what he wants. Consequently, they will constantly have to keep themselves 'fit as a fiddle' and ready for love."

"What about kissing other than as a sexual preliminary after an invitation has been accepted?"

"It must come to an end, along with handshaking, because the person who makes the first gesture is judging that this is desired by the other; but what happens when the other does not wish to extend himself in this direction?"

"He's right, Charlie. It's the same situation as asking questions. The person who makes the gesture knows he is in the wrong, and since it cannot satisfy him to be rejected when there is no way he can compel this response, he leaves well enough alone."

"This means that the only kind of greeting that will remain in existence is something like 'Hi' and 'Goodbye,' 'So long,' 'See you later,' etc., simply because none of these require any response. To expect one blames someone in advance for not doing what is expected."

"But wouldn't he expect her to prepare the best meals possible?"

"He certainly would, just as she will expect him to do everything in his power to make her happy. However, this is not a judgment of what is right for her because he knows she wants to do this for him, and he would never blame her if she prepared the worst meals. In other words, she knows it would be wrong to fail in this regard because it would be a definite hurt, and it cannot satisfy her to hurt him when she not only loves him but knows he would never criticize her."

"You really did it, Larry! I can't see any flaw at all; can you, Charlie?"

"I can't see how any boy or girl marrying under these conditions could ever desire to leave the other for another lover since it would be mathematically impossible (he's got me saying it) for them to ever fall out of love. But how is it possible to ever get such a world started? This is going to be your stumbling block."

"Don't worry about it. It is humorous to observe that in our present world, a husband and wife blame each other for any unhappiness in their marriage because they are unaware of who or what really struck the first blow. By revealing what it means that man's will is not free, which releases the corollary or basic principle (magic elixir, if you will) that no person is to blame, every individual becomes conscious that he alone is responsible for any hurt done to himself by his marital partner, just as long as she knows there will be no blame and that advance blame strikes the first blow. You are beginning to see the infinite wisdom that governs this universe of human relations through invariable laws when you realize there is no law that can compel a man to live with and support a woman, if he makes up his mind that anything else is better; but of what value is having this law when he, of his own free will, can never desire to leave under the changed conditions? The services of a rabbi and priest during a marriage ceremony don't come to an end because these include the inculcation of a couple's obligations to each other, which is a form of advance blame, but only because the boy and girl, at this stage of man's development, are getting married in a superior manner, which renders this service obsolete. However, it is important for boys and girls to know what is and is not a hurt. Think further about this immense wisdom (these invariable laws of God). At the very moment it is revealed what love actually is... nothing other than a strong desire for sexual satisfaction (as if we really didn't know), we are prevented from having more than one sexual partner all through life, while being allowed to fall in love with any number of people who could satisfy this passion, just by making us aware of what it means that our eyes are not a sense organ and that man's will is not free. This entire knowledge compels a couple, when they realize that no more favors will ever be asked, to ask: 'Honey, is there anything I can do for you?' And the other, not wishing to take advantage of such a generous offer because to do so would not be an advantage since this would not reveal their love, replies, in 99% of the cases, 'No thank you,' which means that this question never needs to be asked. If either one has something that cannot be done alone (excluding sex), they would simply request the assistance of the other, who would never object because no advantage was being taken. This would be the one percent."

"This whole thing is simply fantastic, incredible!"

"I agree, Charlie, but what about the marriages that are already here? And what about homosexuals?"

"In a relatively short period of time, only the new marriages will be in existence. As for homosexuals, they are free to find a partner without blame. This is their business. However, all homosexuals that came into existence as a result of environmental conditions, not inherited or glandular, will be compelled to fall by the wayside — in due time."

CHAPTER EIGHT
CHARLIE'S SUBTLE PLAN

Just as the word time was uttered, the phone rang. It was Charlie's boss. An emergency had arisen on the West Coast, and he was ordered to go there immediately for at least two months. He apologized to Larry, although it was not necessary, and begged him to wait until he returned before showing the rest of the blueprint. He called Alice immediately to tell her that he was leaving within two hours.

"Hello," said a very unhappy voice.

"What's wrong, Honey? You sound terrible. Harry isn't home, is he?"

"Am I glad you called. He just walked out and slammed the door. I finally told him about us. I had to. I can't take this marriage any longer, and since he wouldn't consider a divorce for any other reason, I thought that if I told him about us, he might get mad enough to give it to me. Instead, he ordered me to be out of the house by the end of one hour and said that if I wasn't, he would pick me up and throw me out bodily. 'And you might as well forget about that divorce,' he yelled as he left. I'm afraid of him, and I have nowhere to go."

"Get your stuff together, call a cab, and get right over here. I know this is not what you really want, but we have no choice under the circumstances. Besides, I'm leaving immediately for California on a business trip for at least two months, so you can have the entire apartment to yourself."

As he hung up the receiver, he got a brainstorm right out of the blue. Since he knew that the principles in Larry's manuscript were mathematically undeniable, it dawned on him that if he could get Alice's husband to read the manuscript, Harry would have no reason not to give her the divorce. "If only I could get Larry to lend it to me."

"Listen, Larry, I was just thinking. Since I would like to go over everything you explained thus far, and since I will have plenty of time traveling to and from California, could you let me borrow your manuscript to take on the trip? I know you have at least one more, and I would take very good care of it, I assure you."

"I don't mind. And we'll pick up where we left off when you return."

"I must start packing right away, so you guys will have to excuse me. Thanks again, Larry. I'll call you the moment I get back."

About thirty minutes after they left, Alice walked in carrying two suitcases.

"Honey, I've got the greatest news, that is, if you still want a divorce."

"Are you kidding? You know I do."

"Well, listen very carefully because I have a terrific plan. Do you see this manuscript? It contains the most powerful knowledge ever written. It will soon be read by, or taught to, everybody in the entire world, just as soon as Larry... you met him once... gets it published and starts the ball rolling. But he hasn't completed his work yet. Anyway, if you want to get your divorce, all you have to do is get your husband to read these eight chapters, but first I want you to read them so you will be able to at least give him an intelligent answer should he question you in any way. As a last resort, just in case he doesn't want to read it and since he's always looking for investment opportunities, tell him that you thought he might be interested in it from a publishing standpoint. But if you want your divorce, you must get him to read it. Here's my phone number in Burbank. Let me know what happens. If I don't hear from you, I'll see you when I return. So long, Doll."

"Do you have to leave this minute? You'll be gone for two months, and we have the whole place to ourselves."

"I really wish I had more time, but I have to rush, Doll. I'll be back before you know it, and we'll have a lifetime together, with or without that divorce. So long, baby. I'll see you in about two months."

He kissed her real long, and then dashed out. She sat quietly for a few minutes with her thoughts, feeling very much alone, and then decided to start reading. She read into the wee hours of the morning. "I do believe Charlie is right. Harry may give me a divorce at that." She waited three days before deciding to visit him. Then she called the house to make sure he was there, and when he answered, she hung up. She immediately called a cab, and with the manuscript under her arm, she got out of the taxi one block from the house. She was so afraid of what her husband was liable to say or do when he saw her that to help overcome her fears she started singing, "Happy days are here again, da.da..da da..da da.. da da." But in spite of her singing, she felt terrible, although she looked as if she were happy. Finally, she got up enough courage to knock on the door and smile.

"What do you want, you rotten whore? And what are you so happy about? You might as well forget that divorce because I'll never let you marry that gigolo, that wife stealer. If you think for one minute that you can ruin my life, make me miserable, you lousy prostitute, and then expect me to help you find happiness, you have another thought coming. When I die, that's when you'll get your freedom, you dirty bitch. So don't bother coming over to see if I have changed my mind. Do you think I ever loved you? I hate your rotten guts. Now get out of here... and take all your clothes before I call the police to arrest you for dirtying up my steps."

"Wait a minute, Harry; don't close the door yet. I didn't come over to ask that you give me a divorce. I know it is useless. I brought something for you to read that I thought you might find interesting because you are a religious person who believes in God. That's true, isn't it?"

She was praying that he would answer, at least to keep him from closing the door. He opened it a little wider and said:

"You know I am a devout Catholic. Didn't I go to church every Sunday, and didn't I always insist that you join me and the children? But you preferred playing tennis from early morning to sundown. How the neighbors talked!"

"What's done is done, Harry, and you don't have to live with me anymore. Anyway, the author of this manuscript has positive proof that God will reveal Himself to all mankind by performing a miracle. He actually demonstrates how God comes down from heaven in the form of a mathematical revelation and puts an end to all evil in the world. He further proves that no one is to blame for anything because man's will is not free, which makes God, who was building a house for his children to live in, although not completed yet (the roof still has to be put on), responsible for everything."

"Man's will is not free! God is responsible for the evil in the world!? What in the hell are you talking about? Do you mean that God is to blame for your adultery, for my not wanting to give you a divorce because it is against my religion, and because you're a no-good rat that I would like to make miserable? He is to blame for my hating your rotten guts, not you? Is that what you mean?"

"Not exactly, but sort of. It's all here in these sheets. The theme is sort of a game for two people. I will never blame you anymore for not wanting to give me a divorce and for calling me all those nasty names, and you won't blame me for wanting one. You know, tit for tat."

"Is this why you came over here, to give me that crap to read? You must be some kind of nut. After ruining my life, you don't want to be blamed because God is responsible; therefore, I should let you off the hook, right? Isn't that what you really want? No wonder you like this author, but you're both nuts. You can take those sheets and use them for toilet paper or stick them up... you know where. God is all goodness, and you, a rat born of the devil (I hope your mother forgives me), want to blame our Lord for your sins, for giving your body to someone else after we promised not to, in holy wedlock. Get out of here. I can't stand the sight of you."

And again, he started to close the door.

"But wait, Harry, just one more minute. Please don't close the door yet."

She was afraid to mention anything about him publishing it because of what he might do, so she had to try and explain herself.

"I'm not blaming God because I didn't have to do those things that hurt you so much, if I didn't want to, but God made me want to. You see, there was a purpose to all evil; therefore, you shouldn't blame me for committing adultery and wanting to marry someone I love very much. In the new world, on Judgment Day, that is, when all judgment ceases, you will never hold this against me. Believe me, I wouldn't blame you for anything you did, even if you smacked me, because I know that you can't help yourself since man's will is not free. I realize how this must sound, but it's true."

"Where in the hell did the author pick up all that crap? The Catholic religion teaches that man's will is definitely free. He must be a real goofball, that guy. But he's perfectly right about one thing. I am definitely not to blame, because you are. You committed adultery, not me. You didn't have to eat my heart out like you did in so many ways, hurt me to the core, even hurt the children by becoming a cheap slut. He's right; you did it only because you wanted to, and now I'm going to get even. Your conscience is bothering you; that's why you came over."

"That's true; I don't like what I've done, but I want to do the decent thing and get married. I'm really sorry about all that happened, but I could not help falling in love with Charlie. It was just one of those things."

"I know the very thing you are talking about, and I'm not blaming you. But I can't help myself either because God is making me make you suffer like you made me suffer. Now get out of here along with that other goofball."

And again, he started to close the door.

"Just one second more, Harry. Maybe I'm not explaining it right, but some scientist, I can't think of his name" (she was reaching for anything), "said it is a fantastic, mathematical discovery direct from the horse's mouth, God himself."

Realizing that this was not the thing to say, after she said it, she tried to take it back.

"I didn't mean..."

"Never mind what you meant. The very fact that you can talk like that about our Lord shows me what kind of a nut you really are. You will be punished one day for such disrespect."

"Don't take me so literally. Anyway, this revelation is supposed to make everybody happy by creating an entirely new and better world — once they understand the basic principle, advance blame, and the fact that man does not have five senses."

"Doesn't have five senses! Jesus Christ, what are you going to say next?"

"Maybe it is a little over my head, but it still made me happy. It can't hurt you to read it, and since you are unhappy, maybe it will do the trick for you, too."

"Are you concerned for my happiness? Is that why you want me to read it? Well, drown yourself, and I'll be happy. You must have some ulterior motive, and more than likely it is another attempt to convince me to give you a divorce. The only thing you said so far that makes sense is that it might be over your head. You never were too intelligent and never got much of an education. In fact, you never even finished high school. My father, God rest his soul, told me you were absolutely nothing but good-looking and that I would be making a big mistake, especially after my little sister checkmated you in six moves. He could never understand what I saw in you, and now I really wonder myself."

For the first time, Alice realized how she could reach him.

"I admit I'm not too bright and that I should have at least completed high school. Perhaps that's why I really do not understand the author and am making him appear like some kind of nut. However, forget it. My real purpose in coming over was not to get you to change your mind about the divorce (you made it emphatically clear three days ago that I would never get one), but to interest you in a business proposition. After studying the knowledge in this manuscript, you might want to be the publisher, and if so, I would like a royalty. Supposing the author really has something, wouldn't you like to give yourself the benefit of the doubt and read what he has? How would you feel if someone else made the fortune you could have made?"

She could tell by his expression that she had him.

"I won't make any promises about how much your cut will be until I have read it, assuming that I want it then.

But you can leave the manuscript. Don't bother me anymore about a divorce, is that understood?"

Despite his last words and all the abuse, Alice had accomplished her purpose, and she felt absolutely certain that it would do the trick, but mainly because Charlie said so. Five weeks later she decided to give Harry a call, realizing that he had no way of getting in touch with her if he decided to.

"Hello!"

"Harry, this is Alice. Did you get a chance to read the manuscript?"

"I sure did, and I can't thank you enough! I've decided to publish it and have already contacted the author. I'll work out something satisfactory with you, as your end. And incidentally, I've decided to give you a divorce..."

She nearly fell off the chair.

"Are you serious?"

"I most certainly am, but under one condition."

"What is that?"

"I insist that you come over here and live with me for two weeks, under the conditions described in the manuscript. After that, you are a free woman. I can't be more fair than that."

"If I should decide to accept, I wouldn't be under any obligation to make love, would I?"

"You wouldn't be under any kind of obligation because this is advance blame, remember, and I won't tell you anything to do, or ask any favors. You will be free to do anything you want to do. Call me back in a few minutes if you decide to come over. These are my terms."

She immediately put in a long-distance call to Charlie.

"Hello!"

"Jim, it worked! He's going to give me a divorce!"

"That's the greatest news, and I'll be home in ten days, maybe in seven."

"But there's a condition to the divorce, that's why I'm calling."

"What kind of condition?"

"He insists that I live with him for the next two weeks, according to the principles of Larry's knowledge. He's expecting me to call him right back if I decide."

"What's another two weeks? You'll be free of him then, once and for all."

"But I can't stand being around him for two whole weeks. Just his fatness gets on my nerves. Besides, when you get home, should I agree to it, I'll still be over his house."

"Alice, listen. It's only for two weeks, so stop worrying. Remember, you don't have to get in bed with him unless you want to, since he can't place you under any kind of obligation, not according to Larry's principles. You don't even have to sleep in the same room. Stop worrying and think only about getting married and living happily ever after. I can't wait to see you, Honey, and I love you very much."

"I love you too, Charlie. All right, then; I'll call him back to tell him that I have agreed. Call me when you get home."

She immediately phoned Harry.

"Yes…"

"It's me again, Harry. I've accepted the terms. When do you want me to come over?"

THE SECRET

"I've decided to take off the next two weeks, starting tomorrow. Come out anytime you want."

The next morning, with her two suitcases (Harry had forgotten that she had all her winter clothes stored, and even the cedar closet in the basement was still filled with her things), she went over in a cab. She really dreaded the next two weeks but made up her mind to stand it. As she approached the door, she remembered how he had called her such names only five weeks ago, but when he answered the door, never in a million years did she expect to see such a complete transformation.

After studying the principles very carefully, which he understood thoroughly, he decided to give his marriage one more chance by getting back into the shape he was in when she first met him and by doing everything in accordance with the principles. Consequently, he went on a blitz diet and did several things to reduce his weight. So, when she saw him standing at the door, it was like seeing a ghost out of the past because the man who stood in front of her strongly resembled the person with whom she fell in love many years ago.

"Hi Alice! Let me take your bags."

They had always slept in a double bed, but Harry had arranged a room completely for herself. He even sent the kids away to his brother's farm. That evening, after the housekeeper left, he asked if there was anything he could do for her, but she simply said, "No thank you." She decided to put him to a little test because the condition was that she stay in the house with him for two weeks, so a little later she remarked:

"I'm going out for a while, do you mind?"

"I want you to know again, Alice, that I loved every bit of that knowledge. It is exactly what you said — 'a mathematical revelation.' Consequently, you don't have to ask my permission for anything. Even though the agreement was that you stay in the house with me for two weeks, and even though I wouldn't want you to leave right now, as this would be a hurt to me, still, I won't hold it against you, and you will get your divorce regardless, after the two weeks."

For the first time, Alice got an actual taste of how this basic principle worked. She felt guilty because she had agreed to the terms and now wanted to change them, for which he was not blaming her.

"Never mind, it wasn't that important. I wanted to get a sundae at the drugstore."

"Do you still like the same flavor?"

"Yes, I do."

"I'll order it for you on the phone. Is there anything else you would like?"

"Nothing, thank you."

After eating their sundaes quietly... neither said a word. Harry went into his room and came out wearing the sexiest, translucent robe Alice had ever seen. He looked like a male prostitute. She felt a little embarrassed, but because she knew that he was extending an invitation and because she felt a twinge of excitement and did not want to be intimate with him, she went to her room and stayed there for the night. This went on for four days. On the fifth, he was really tortured. He was so hungry for a sexual relationship that he wondered if he could stay away for the entire remaining time without attacking her, but she was beginning to feel the pressure herself. It had been almost seven weeks since she went to bed with Charlie, and she was accustomed to making love pretty often. That evening, rather than just wear his sexy outfit and do nothing else, he partially opened up his robe so she could see his penis and then began to squirm. He then said to her:

"Alice, I know I never did this to you before, but I sure would like to suck your juicy honey pot. I could suck on it for an hour. I could kiss your entire body all over. Boy, would I like to stick my tongue inside your precious, precious honey pot."

She was shocked. He was using some kind of lotion that put her in the mood. She began to reason with herself. "Even if we make love, this doesn't mean I can't go back to Charlie. Besides, I won't even tell him about it. But I would sure like to suck his dick." But in spite of everything she said to herself, she couldn't get up enough nerve to accept his invitation. She still remembered that he considered such things perverted acts. She just couldn't believe this was her husband. She finally went to her room again, and he thought he had lost her for another night, but soon she came out wearing a sexy negligee. She sat down on the couch opposite him, opened up her legs, and said:

"Come on, Harry; you can suck my honey pot all night if you want to."

He couldn't believe his ears. He was so hot he almost had an orgasm then and there. He tried to appear calm, but he was almost trembling from passion. They fucked and sucked each other for two hours, and for the first time, he actually came two times. He made her come three times by sucking on it, and two times by fucking her. And when they were finished, it wasn't like before when she wanted to sleep on the sofa. He would always say, "You know I can't sleep without you, so why are you so selfish? Why do you insist on sleeping by yourself?" Instead, she went to her room, and he to his. The next morning, she was in the mood all over again, but his door was closed. To open it without being invited to do so was advance blame and under the conditions of what she wanted, so was knocking on the door. Instead, she went down to lie on the sofa and wait for him. It was the housekeeper's day off, so she didn't mind wearing her negligee. When he came downstairs wearing his street clothes and saw her pussy staring him in the face, he felt like softly nibbling it. Since he knew she was extending him an invitation — although he could have ignored it without an explanation — he walked right over and started kissing her tits, her stomach, and then her honey pot. She opened his fly and began to play sixty-nine. By the end of nine days, they were so much in love with each other all over again that Alice knew she could never go back to Charlie, especially since she would now have her children again, and there was no more chance for arguments. She realized that going back to him would be a hurt to her husband (her children were already hurt by her leaving), as well as a hurt to herself, since this is not what she really preferred. By not going back to Charlie, she knew this would hurt him, but she had no choice under the circumstances because she was compelled to choose what gave her greater satisfaction. When he phoned, she told him the news. A few days later, Larry and Jim met again with Charlie at his apartment.

"Congratulations! I understand that you already have a publisher, even before completing your work."

"Thanks to you. Harry told me everything. I'm sorry things didn't work out, but in this particular case, it was inevitable."

"I didn't think you were trying to tell me that this must happen in all cases."

"Of course not, but before long, only the new type of marriages will be in existence. However, for you to more fully appreciate the changes about to take place in our already existing marriages, I shall return to this subject after certain things are explained regarding the economic world, which is next on the agenda."

SEYMOUR LESSANS

PART THREE
THE EXTENSION OF THESE PRINCIPLES
INTO THE ECONOMIC WORLD
CHAPTER NINE — INCEPTION OF THE GOLDEN
AGE
CHAPTER TEN — THE DISPLACED
CHAPTER ELEVEN — THE WISDOM OF
SOCRATES

CHAPTER NINE
INCEPTION OF THE GOLDEN AGE

"Before we get started, I would like to know if dirty words will be used in the new world?"

"If you can tell me the difference between vagina and pussy, penis and dick, sexual intercourse and fuck, I will answer your question, Charlie."

"The one group of words pertains to an objective description, while the other is subjective and emotionally involves the user."

"That was pretty good, Larry."

"Now tell me, is anybody being hurt by the use of these words?"

"Certain people are judged very critically if they are involved in them and other things, like the President and his family. They have to adhere to the strictest protocol, and if it were known that they used such language or looked at dirty books, the people would look down on them, perhaps not even vote for them."

"In other words, the hurt is this judging of what is right for others, which has already been established as wrong. Consequently, the moment people are compelled to refrain from criticizing others when there is no one being hurt — because all criticism is a form of hurt for which they know they will not be blamed — then the real hurt, not these words, must come to an end. But you will understand this much better when I get to education and discuss other words... the ones that really hurt. Can I get started now?"

"I'm satisfied with your answer."

"In order to solve a problem, even with our basic principle, it is absolutely necessary to understand what we are faced with, and in the economic world, there are three aspects of hurt. The first is not being able to fulfill our basic needs. The second is the inability to maintain the standard of living that was developed. And the last is to be denied an opportunity, if desired, to improve one's standard of living. However, before I demonstrate how this hurt is removed, it is necessary to remind you, at this juncture, that will is not free because man never has a choice, as with aging, and then it is obvious that he is under the normal compulsion of living regardless of what his particular motion at any moment might be, or he has a choice, and then is given two or more alternatives of which he is compelled, by his very nature, to prefer the one that gives him greater satisfaction, whether it is the lesser of two evils, the greater of two goods, or a good over an evil.

It is also necessary to observe that when man is compelled to give up his desire to hurt others, which is evil, because he knows there will be no blame, he is not choosing the greater of two goods or the lesser of two evils, but a good over an evil. But if by not hurting others he makes matters worse for himself, then he is compelled to prefer the lesser of two evils, and this is what happens where the first two aspects of hurt are concerned. In other words, if we find ourselves unable to get what we need, then we are compelled to blame and even hurt those who have it. Employees who find their income falling short of the mark because of rising prices blame their employer for having too much money and strike to take some of it away. The employer, in turn, who has discovered that the strike has lowered his income, and the government, finding itself unable to meet its needs under the present tax structure, blame the people for having too much money and decide to take some of it away by increasing prices and taxes. The people, falling below their needs because of this increase, blame the government and anybody else they can cheat to get back what they lost. The manufacturers, wholesalers, and retailers are compelled to lay off their surplus employees when consumption slows down, and to prevent this, since there is no way the United States can consume all it produces, the government is forced to do everything humanly possible to keep its foreign markets open and reduce unnecessary competition; otherwise, a recession and perhaps depression could result. But war keeps millions of people employed, reduces the already overcrowded earth and the chances of a depression, so what is the better choice? Everywhere we look, man is compelled to prefer the lesser of two evils, and under this condition, our basic principle can have no effect. Therefore, to solve our problem, since this is the kind of situation that exists in the economic world, it is necessary to remove the first blow. In other words, if A is compelled to hurt B because the alternative of not doing this is still worse, then A has no choice but to hurt B, as when the unions strike, when prices and taxes are increased, when layoffs occur, when the government prefers war, etc. But if there is no possibility for it to make matters worse for himself by not hurting B, then this aspect of justification has been removed, and it then becomes possible to prevent man from desiring to hurt others when he knows there will be no blame, which compels him, beyond his control, to choose a good (not to hurt anybody) over an evil (to do so). Now the question arises at this point: How can we create an environment that would remove the conditions that make it necessary to select the lesser of two evils as a solution to our problems?"

"I really don't know, especially since you already said that the basic principle cannot be used here."

"Are you sure you don't know, Charlie, or are you just being modest?"

"Don't be funny, Jim."

"It can't be used in a positive sense, but it can in a negative sense. Let me explain what I mean. If someone was hurt and yelling, 'Help! Help! Help!', and you were in a position to render assistance without hurting yourself while knowing that you would never be blamed if you didn't, is it humanly possible for you to find satisfaction in ignoring this cry, especially if you know absolutely and positively that all mankind, should you ever find yourself in a similar position, would never fail to help you?"

"Under such conditions, I believe that Jim and I, as well as others, would desire to help this individual."

"Well, believe it or not, this is the key to the economic solution. Since we have already established the two conditions that strike the first blow of hurt, and since those who fall below their standard of living, along with those who cannot acquire the necessaries of life, are hurt (drowning, so to speak) and yelling for help but will never blame us if we don't because they know we can't help ourselves — although I know we can if we want to, for over this I will demonstrate that we have mathematical control — we are given no choice but to unite in such a way, without blaming anybody for anything because everything developed out of mathematical necessity, that all mankind notwithstanding, will be guaranteed against the possibility of this hurt. Then, by allowing everybody complete freedom to improve their standard of living without the slightest fear of punishment or retaliation, they would be compelled of their own free will to prefer good, that is, not starting anything evil, because no satisfaction can be gotten otherwise under the changed conditions."

"This sounds good, if nothing else, and you seem to have all the answers, but how is it possible to meet the extra cost of raising all those who are not receiving the necessaries of life to this basic standard, plus meeting the entire guarantee? If 50 billion dollars were needed for one week, and all that could be raised without anybody going below his standard was 30 billion, you're in trouble. And what about those who cannot understand what it means that man's will is not free, which knowledge is necessary to prevent a hurt when man is given his freedom? He must understand the principles in order to consider this hurt to others the worse possible choice. And even if he does understand, but your guarantee fails to work because there is just not enough money (labor), he would be compelled, as a motion in the direction of greater satisfaction, to take advantage of not being blamed to select the lesser of two evils, that is, to take what he needs from others, one way or another, rather than go below his standard. Furthermore, guaranteeing his standard of living is a negative benefit if he is not at all satisfied with it, which means that he might prefer the insecurity of going below, as a gambler will do, to the security, which could deny him the opportunity of improving. But even giving you the benefit of the doubt — that the principles can be taught, the guarantee made to work, and the overall benefits will be positive as well as negative — how is it humanly possible to get such a world started when communism and capitalism have opposing ideologies? Last but far from least, what do you mean by a standard of living?"

"Take it easy, Charlie. I realize the whole thing seems impossible, but let me answer all your questions by proceeding in a systematic manner. Now, once the leaders of every nation are convinced that the blueprint of this solution is scientifically undeniable (we shall assume this for the moment in order to move along), they will set up IBM computer offices, or the equivalent, for the purpose of making this guarantee work. These offices will be related to IBM centers, as cities to states, and these centers will be tied together with the International Bureau of Internal Revenue. When this has been completed, a written test will be made up as an entrance examination on the principles involved, which must be passed by those interested in becoming citizens of the GOLDEN AGE before receiving the guarantee. However, the leaders and all those in government who are associated with them in any capacity where blaming others is a part of their job (remember, everything is exactly the same except for the written test and the IBM offices), the greatest transition in the history of mankind will be well on its way."

"Everything you say brings up questions."

"I'll let Charlie do the talking."

"Why must this group take their examination first? Supposing someone doesn't pass, would he not be entitled to the guarantee and be compelled to live in the old world where he must face the possibility of going below his standard of living and choose, as a solution to his problem, the lesser of two evils?"

"Just as parents must assume responsibility for a child until he is able to understand the principles, so likewise will someone have to assume responsibility for anyone who does not pass in order for this guarantee to be issued. However, it is not that difficult to learn what has to be, and the clergy will strongly desire to spread word of the new gospel that will soon put an end to all evil, even though this means the eventual end of all religion, since no one will have the need to spend their money in that direction. The truth is very easy to understand because it involves undeniable relations, such as two plus two equals four; but when people have been taught, out of necessity, that man's will is free and his eyes a sense organ, it becomes more difficult to break through this sound barrier of learned, unconscious ignorance because the long tenure of preempted authority has confused opinions with facts and dogmatically closed the door to further investigation. However, when theologians fully realize not only that they were teaching something false and that God's will, the truth, was hidden behind that door but that their standard of living will be permanently guaranteed, we will very quickly get their cooperation in attaining this sonic boom. Now the reason the leaders of the world and their subordinates must take their examination first is because it is only by knowing he will never be blamed by them or the laws of their country, no matter what he does to hurt others, that the new citizen can be prevented from desiring to do that for which punishment came into existence, taking for granted, of course, that the other source of justification, this being made to go below his standard of living, has already been removed."

"But couldn't such an arrangement present quite a problem — the fact that some would be citizens while others are not? How is it possible for the basic principle to prevent him from desiring to hurt noncitizens in order to gain an advantage when he knows they will blame, criticize, retaliate, etc., if he is caught, even though he knows the laws will not punish him? If this should occur, wouldn't this compel these noncitizens to take the laws into their own hands?"

"There is absolutely no way a citizen could find satisfaction in hurting noncitizens when his standard of living is guaranteed never to go down and when he knows, well in advance, that the laws of his nation must excuse him for doing what he can never justify. This will compel him to think like never before in order to prevent any possible hurt to others."

"But what about the hurt to him by noncitizens? Is he justified to retaliate, or must he turn the other cheek?"

"He is perfectly justified to defend himself, but it must be remembered that the laws of a nation will remain in force just as long as there are people who have not passed their examination; consequently, he does not have to turn the other cheek, and this allows the transition to proceed without fear, even though he would be living in two worlds."

"What about prisoners; will they be allowed to take the examination? And if they pass, will this give them their freedom, regardless of what they were in prison for?"

"Certainly, because it will be mathematically impossible, under the changed conditions, for them to ever desire hurting others again. But just as the leaders of the world were first in taking the examination, so the prisoners will be among the last."

"What determines priority? And supposing a prisoner is awaiting execution, but because of being last, he can't possibly become a citizen before the day on which he is scheduled to die; what happens then?"

"Once the transition gets officially launched, that is, once the leaders have set up their IBM offices and become citizens by passing their examination, they will forthwith abolish capital punishment. As for priority, this is determined by those whose jobs, professions, or businesses will be displaced first by the transition."

"It seems to me that noncitizens could take advantage of the knowledge that they would be released from prison after passing their examination, should they get caught breaking the law. They could kill someone hated very much and not fear the charge. They could successfully rob a bank of a million dollars, hide the money, and, if caught, take their examination and be released to enjoy the fruit of their plan. Something doesn't seem just right."

"Remember, man must always do what he thinks is better for himself, which compels the noncitizen to take into consideration the possible consequences. In trying to kill somebody, he himself could become the victim. He could also be killed while attempting to rob the bank. Furthermore, he must also weigh the possible years he could spend in prison just waiting for his turn to take the examination, which he might fail, with no one willing to assume responsibility in his case. He might also be executed before the transition is officially launched. You have looked at a negative possibility without comparing the positive benefits to the potential citizen, who is now a free man looking in, not looking out. And because the comparison gives no free choice, everybody, notwithstanding who gets wind of this new world, so to speak, will desire to become a citizen just as soon as possible."

"But what about gangsters, racketeers, gamblers, bookmakers — those who are paid to commit murder? What about the dope peddlers?"

"Anybody who makes his living by doing something that hurts others, which does not include gambling, has a choice to make. He can pass his examination and become a citizen, which guarantees his standard of living and allows him to change his job without being a loser, or he can continue to hurt others to earn his income, with the constant possibility of earning less while ending up in prison. Is he really given a choice? As for those who make their living through gambling, there is absolutely no hurt involved whatsoever.

Horse racing is a business; so is the stock market. Nobody forces a person to place a bet or invest his money; he does this of his own free will. If he loses, he has nobody to blame but himself. Consequently, the moment these bookmakers become citizens, they are free forevermore from the trammels of the law."

"But supposing someone gambles away his income to such a degree that he falls below his standard of living, or suppose the bookmaker who is earning one hundred thousand a year goes broke; are we supposed to give them the money to make up the deficit? And what about the dope peddler?"

"Once a pusher becomes a citizen, he will lose the desire to continue earning his living that way, that is, to push the sale of his products with misleading information, which means that once all available facts about drugs are made public and all blame withdrawn, the user will find very little satisfaction in taking this chance of hurting himself, but if he wants to, that's his business. The citizen will not find any satisfaction in remaining in a business that hurts others under the changed conditions, and the noncitizen, knowing that his standard of living is guaranteed when he becomes a citizen, and realizing that just as long as he continues to engage in illegal activities, he is subject to the full penalty of the laws, cannot wait to study and pass his examination."

"Are you trying to say that all drugs will be legal and sold in stores?"

"I will answer this more thoroughly in a little while, but don't jump to any conclusions. As for gambling that hurts others by too great a loss, how is this possible when he is well aware, in advance, that they will never blame him for this hurt? But this, too, along with why it will be mathematically impossible for anybody to take advantage of the guarantee, you will understand much better very shortly."

"You made the prediction that all war will come to a permanent end between 1975 and 1980. Doesn't this require that all mankind be citizens, and wouldn't this be stretching your hopes quite a bit?"

"Not at all. Once the leaders and their subordinates, which include the armed forces of the world, become citizens, it will be mathematically impossible for war to continue or begin again. Only noncitizens could desire to start something, but until they pass their examination — and this they will be anxious to do — they will be controlled by the laws of their country and the combined citizens of the world. Consequently, each country would retain its armed forces, which would be reduced in just proportion as the noncitizens decrease, as a precautionary measure."

"What about the possibility of a general passing his examination and then becoming mentally ill with a desire to rule the world? Or, what if any citizen struck a first blow of hurt?"

"Anytime a citizen would hurt somebody physically or give a command to hurt others as the general might, we would know immediately that he was sick and would commit him to a hospital until he is able to resume his normal life. We would do the same if a dog were to bite somebody — take him off the street. However, even though it is very unlikely that a citizen would become mentally ill under the changed conditions, we would be prepared for any eventuality. It is taken for granted that it will be impossible for him to derive any satisfaction from doing what is wrong because there would be no blame or punishment, which means that the solution is simply to show him what is right at the time he takes his examination, and the line of demarcation is mathematically drawn. But everything will become crystal clear as the guarantee is brought into play.

Now, a standard of living is the available services and materials that an individual can purchase with his or her net income. It is the amount left over after all deductible items and taxes have been subtracted from the gross, less his personal insurance premiums. In other words, if someone earned an average of $250 a week, spent $50 of this on deductible items that have nothing to do with taxes of any kind, another $50 on taxes which include federal, state, social security, excise, licenses, property, and anything I might have omitted, and $20 on personal insurance coverage, then his standard of living would be estimated at $130 a week. This means that if this particular citizen ever found himself in a position whereby he could not find a job or one paying the amount needed, which is $130 in this case, and had absolutely no cash reserve or potential to help himself (this includes bonds, cash from his life insurance and anything that can be converted to cash, but which does not play a role in his standard of living such as a car), then we, those of us in a position to help without hurting ourselves, that is, without going below our own guarantee, would desire to offer him this money by contributing an equal share to maintain his standard or raise him to the basic level, so that he would never have to take away from others what he needs by resorting to strikes, price increases, war to control foreign markets, taxation, crime or anything else done to hurt others as the lesser of two evils."

"Why did you deduct insurance premiums when this is not a deductible item except as a business expense, especially when insurance definitely plays a role in maintaining one's standard of living?"

"You must constantly bear in mind that when someone comes to us for help, he must be absolutely broke. If we were to make his guarantee $150 instead of $130 so that he could invest the $20 with insurance companies, we would be increasing the cost of the overall guarantee by the amount that was not used. In other words, if the total insurance premiums amounted to one hundred million dollars but only fifty were used by the insurance companies to pay off the various damages, then we increased our cost of the guarantee by 50 million. Besides, he was already covered when the $20 was deducted to arrive at his standard of living, which means that if he lost his house by fire and had absolutely nothing with which to help himself, we would not only rebuild its value but incur all other expenses necessary to maintain his standard of living."

"I can understand this, but by not providing him the money to insure himself with these companies, you would have to hurt them."

"How is it possible to hurt them when their standard of living — each member of every company who is a citizen — is guaranteed? Are you implying that we are supposed to continue having crime because the manufacturers of burglar alarms need the criminal to earn a living? We are not going to guarantee their job or business which depends on buyers for what they have to sell; just their net income when they are completely or partially displaced."

"But this brings up a very interesting point where the non-displaced are concerned regarding insurance. Knowing that he is covered by the guarantee, why should this citizen continue investing $20 in insurance when he could put it to better use?"

"Simply because to stop would be taking advantage of the guarantee, and there is no advantage when this could result in an increase to our cost, for which hurt there would be no blame."

"Well, let me rephrase my question: Supposing this displaced person, after letting his policies lapse because he couldn't keep them up, gets a new job paying $250, but now he has no insurance because he was forced to use up the cash from his life insurance and drop all other policies. Is he supposed to reinvest the $20 in insurance coverage, even though he is already covered by the guarantee?"

"Some of his policies might still be in force, but if he was investing $20 on insurance before getting displaced and he can do this again without going below his own guarantee, then he would desire to do this to prevent a hurt to those who will not only not blame him for this but will help him again if necessary."

"Something else just came to mind that might be related to insurance, and I think I see a flaw. If dropping insurance takes advantage of the guarantee, which cannot be done, wouldn't it also be taking advantage if a person who knows he will soon be displaced and who has a huge reserve in cash and a large guaranteed net income decides to spend it all on luxuries so that he wouldn't have to use it towards sustaining his own guarantee and could then draw what he needs from us? In other words, any person who knows he is going to be displaced would increase the cost of the overall guarantee if he spent his reserve cash on anything that did not pertain to the maintenance of his standard of living. To express it differently, if he had $540 in cash and was going to be displaced for five weeks, this money would cover the entire period if his net income or guarantee was $130 a week. If he spent it on a new television set that broke him instead of using it towards his guarantee, then he would cost us this amount of $130 every week until he gets another job."

"There is no flaw. What he does with his own money is his business, but he must be completely broke before coming to us for help. Remember, he must use up all of his reserve cash before getting help from us, or he would be taking advantage, which would not be an advantage under these conditions."

"What about the $20 a week you said he would have to spend on insurance?"

"For example, if his standard of living was $130 and he was earning, with his new job, $170, but he owed $650 on a previous loan, then he would not be in a position to take out insurance until he has paid off his debt, at which time he would pick up a profit of $20 since the other twenty would be invested on insurance coverage, if that is the amount he was spending at the time he became a citizen."

"But if he feels that there is no way he will ever earn more than what he is presently netting, wouldn't it then be to his advantage, without hurting anybody, to buy the TV set?"

"I repeat: what he does with his own money is his business, but before you make any assumptions, let me show you how everything is done pertaining to the guarantee by going into the IBM office."

"Just one second. Are you trying to tell us that this same system will work regarding people in business for themselves and for those living in a communist country?"

"Everything will be answered shortly, but let me proceed without getting ahead of myself. Now, the moment our friend becomes a citizen, he receives an identification number that is placed on a card with his picture, signature, and guarantee (which is $130 in this case) on metal plates to replace his license tags, and if he has a place of business, on a sheet of paper to replace all other licenses. The $50 he was paying the government in taxes (covering all kinds) will now be sent to his IBM office and recorded on his ledger sheet as a credit, less the amount he spends on personal government services. In other words, any service that is not absolutely essential, or which he does not wish to continue with, will be deducted from the $50 and credited to his account, and this difference will be allocated accordingly, so much for the fire and police departments, for garbage collection, for the maintenance of a traffic system and street repair, etc. If he has no children or prefers a private school, or if he prefers not to use the zoo or park facilities, then he won't have to pay for these, which would increase the amount he can contribute towards the guarantee. Assuming this amount to be $35, it is what would be recorded on his ledger sheet as a credit and would be used only towards the maintenance of the guarantee. If at the end of a year, after becoming a citizen, he has a balance, it would be refunded to him as a profit. The total cost of maintaining the IBM offices and the guarantee would be divided equally among the total number of citizens. If there were 2 billion, and we needed 2 billion dollars for one week, each account would have deducted one dollar. If 3 billion dollars were needed and 500 million could only contribute one dollar without wiping out their account, then the difference would be divided equally among the 1.5 billion citizens."

"But this doesn't seem fair for one reason. If our friend pays in $1820 for the year while someone else pays in $50,000, should an average of $20 a week be used by these citizens, then the one would get back as a profit $780 while the other would receive $48,960. This might be equal, but it is not equitable."

"How is it possible to charge the one man more money without blaming him for his wealth? Is the rich man supposed to pay more for the use of water than the poor man? We cannot do this once all blame is removed. However, if $49,000 of his fifty thousand was used, our friend could not have contributed more than $1820.

"Supposing all the money contributed during one week is inadequate to cover the expense of the guarantee, what happens then?"

"We will use the next week's contribution, the next, and the next. But if at the end of a year we show a deficit, then we would divide the amount needed by the total number of citizens and ask for this contribution. If the amount was 50 billion dollars and we had 2 billion citizens, each would contribute $25, unless this caused some to go below their own guarantee. If so, the difference would be made up by those who could afford it. However, at this point, let me show you what actually takes place. You see, money is used for three things: to buy what we need and want, to invest it in order to have still more money to spend, and to invest it in greater leisure and security. Since the guarantee offers the greatest security imaginable, all money held in reserve or invested towards a greater security can be released. If we spend or invest it, the amount needed for the guarantee (the amount needed for unemployment compensation) will be reduced in just proportion. If we have nothing on which to spend or invest, then it becomes a surplus that will voluntarily be provided to those who need it because they have been displaced and cannot find new jobs as a consequence of our not spending or investing it. What the department store owner does with the extra profit he picks up when the floorwalker is not needed anymore, allowing for the change in the amount of his weekly contribution since this displacement affects it, is strictly his business. The floorwalker, who was compelled to use up all his cash reserve before coming to us for help, dumps into circulation more of the money needed to create new jobs, and every time a displaced person finds new employment, the cost of the guarantee decreases. In other words, if 98% of the government gets displaced eventually because there is no further need for their services, and these people are able to find new jobs that cover, dollar for dollar, the amount we were spending on taxes, then we will create a tremendous profit in our IBM accounts. Furthermore, I am going to demonstrate, in a short while, that prices must come down to a fantastic degree, but first, let me finish showing you what the IBM ledger sheet is used for.

Let's assume that our friend contributed to the guarantee an average of $25 a week for 30 years, at which time he retired with $39,000 credited to his account. If the amount of his net guarantee was affected by the fact that he now does not have any children to support, then the new figure, let us say roughly $100 a week, would be sent to him every week as long as he lives. If he should die before using up all of his credit, his wife would draw the $100 a week, less the amount to be deducted because of his death. If she dies before it is all used up, the balance would be distributed equally among the surviving children — in their IBM accounts. If it is consumed before they die, then they would have to take the amount needed just as long as they live, but all their assets are used to pay off any outstanding debts. If anything is left over, the difference is distributed equally to all their children, dead or alive, in cash. If a child is dead, his wife or her husband gets the share. If the spouse is dead, the children receive it. Everything is auctioned off, but if anything is not sold and more than one child claims it, no partiality can be shown as to who should get what. There will be no more wills because this is a form of discrimination which was necessary in the world of free will, but how is it possible for parents to show partiality when this blames the children for something? If there still exists a deficit after an estate is sold, the account is closed. However, since at the time our friend becomes a citizen, he might be entitled to a certain amount of social security, whatever it is would be figured in as a credit towards his weekly guarantee when he retires. In other words, if, by not paying any more taxes towards his social security (because this money is now going towards the guarantee), he would receive $100 a month at retirement, then this amount will reduce what he consumes of his credit reserve in his IBM account and will reduce the amount he needs to take from us if his credit runs out."

"How can this system work with Russia, one gigantic corporation? And how is it possible to guarantee a businessman his standard of living when competition affects it from week to week?"

"If a person in business draws a set salary every week and settles the difference once a year, then when he applies for his citizenship, the amount of his guarantee and weekly contribution would be based on his figures. If there are any changes, he would estimate the difference because this would affect the amount he contributes, not his guarantee. Now, once all the owners of a particular business become citizens, the price of what they have been selling, whether retail or wholesale, can never be increased because this is a hurt for which there would be no blame. By the same reasoning, the very moment the members of a union become citizens, the cost of their labor can never be raised. This would displace all unions, but they would be given priority to become citizens, just as employees would have priority over employers, manufacturers over wholesalers, and wholesalers over retailers. The citizens who own a retail business and buy from a wholesaler or manufacturer would know that the prices to them would never be increased, which removes the justification to increase prices to the consumer, just as the manufacturer knows that the cost of his labor and materials will never be raised. This means that every person in business will be working on a margin of profit that can only go in one direction — down, and this is what competition and the guarantee will cause to come about. If a retailer is finding it difficult to maintain his standard of living and knows that he cannot come to us for help until he has exhausted all possibilities, then he is compelled to work on a smaller margin of profit. In other words, he must increase his volume, not his prices. By the same reasoning, if the manufacturer and wholesaler are finding it difficult to make ends meet, they, too, have only one possibility open — to reduce their prices to the retailer. If, however, they find it impossible to maintain their standard of living (the wholesaler, manufacturer, and retailer) after consuming all their reserve cash and reducing their profit to the lowest possible margin, they can turn over their entire operation to us and look for another job. We will provide those displaced with the full amount of their guarantee until they get located. Should they decide to sell their business before coming to us, this is their business, but if they can't and need our help, we will take over. Should we sell the business for them, the money would be used to pay off their creditors first, and the remainder would be given to them."

"Supposing they don't clear enough to pay off their creditors?"

"This would be impossible in the new world because at all times, taking everything into consideration, a citizen, employer, or employee will never bite off more than he knows he can chew. If he does, and as a result, he or someone else is forced to come to us for help, we would willingly increase the cost of the overall guarantee without blaming him for doing what he knows we must excuse and he can never justify. Consequently, his accountant will always keep him informed of his credit limitations, unless he can do this himself."

"But this whole thing brings up interesting questions. If someone doesn't like his job, quits, uses up all his cash reserve, and then, because he can't find a job that he likes, comes to us for help; or, to put it another way, supposing a businessman whose standard of living is $500 a week net, decides to sell his business, takes an extended vacation, uses up all his reserve cash, and then gets a job paying only $100 a week gross. Are we supposed to supply the difference?"

"The only time a person can come to us for help, with a clear conscience, that is, is when he loses his job or business involuntarily; otherwise, he would be stealing, for which he knows he would never be blamed. If a businessman cannot maintain his standard of living after reducing his margin of profit to the smallest possible amount, then he is forced to get out."

"Why couldn't he lower the wages of his employees, knowing that the difference would be made up by the guarantee?"

"You should know why, Jim. First, because he would be forcing them to use up their reserve cash, and second, because he would be stealing from the guarantee. Remember, he doesn't have to steal since we are guaranteeing his standard of living, but if he can't make it where he is, then he must get out, assuming that he can earn more elsewhere. If he can't earn more elsewhere, then he would be forced to stay where he is — even though he falls below his standard of living, which will be made up by the guarantee — simply because it is less costly to us."

"But by getting out, if he employs quite a number of people, then this would increase the cost of the guarantee until these people get other comparable jobs. If they don't, then we must supply the difference. Wouldn't it be advisable to subsidize his needs?"

"If he can't sell his products after reducing the profit to the lowest possible margin, then nothing will help him. Besides, we are not going to interfere with economic competition by helping one business, however large or small, rather than another, but we will help all mankind sustain their standard of living."

"Couldn't an employer pay a new employee less than what the job calls for, knowing that the difference would be supplied by the guarantee; and why should it make any difference to the employee whose standard of living is guaranteed?"

"You already asked a similar question. The employer would be stealing this difference from his employee, who would be forced to take it from his IBM office. Nobody will prefer increasing the cost of the guarantee, which means that every displaced person will search for the job that pays the most. If this displaced businessman cannot find a job that meets or exceeds his standard of living, then we would supply the difference."

THE SECRET

"What about corporation taxes?"

"This will be estimated weekly and assigned equitably to the IBM accounts of the stockholders as part of their contribution towards the guarantee. In other words, if a corporation is owned by five stockholders in this manner (10%, 15, 20, 25, and 30%), and the corporate taxes averaged out to $100 a week, then $10, 15, 20, 25, and $30 would be credited to their accounts, respectively. At the end of the year, if it was not used, they would receive it back as a profit, which was already explained."

"What happens to the Bureau of Internal Revenue that now exists?"

"It will be completely displaced in due time. A citizen will continue to use the last tax schedule before passing his examination, as this determines how much he can contribute towards the guarantee, but nobody in the government will be checking what he does. However, because he knows that nobody will blame him no matter how much he cheats, and because he also knows that his own standard of living is guaranteed, he will prefer making sure he does what he judges to be the right thing since no one else will be judging him. And as the citizens increase, the people who work for the Bureau of Internal Revenue will decrease in just proportion."

Right now, an employee has a certain amount deducted from his gross according to a tax table, and at the end of the year, he submits a form that includes the deductible items that allow him to get back a refund."

"This will be changed, and everything will be figured out in advance. If someone got back $520 at the end of the year, then his weekly income would increase by $10. Each citizen would be responsible for mailing in, or dropping off, his own contribution once a week, which means that an employer pays his employees, who are citizens, the gross amount."

"What about liability insurance and hospitalization? I'm still not clear on this and other forms of insurance."

"Since a citizen cannot afford to be careless when he knows there will be no blame, the only insurance he will continue to carry is that which covers any hurt to himself. If a deer darted out in front of his car and caused him to have a collision with another citizen, there would be no blame, and they would take care of their own damages."

"But supposing he ran into the car of a noncitizen?"

"All noncitizens must operate their vehicles according to the laws of their state or city, which means they must carry liability insurance just in case they were at fault, or, if the insurance companies have agreed among themselves to do away with this kind of coverage since it is on its way out, some kind of insurance to take care of the damage to their own car. If this happens to be some form of deductible insurance and the citizen admits he was at fault, even though the deer caused it, then he would pay the amount deducted. If his own insurance company did not cover all the damage and he did not have enough cash reserve, then he knows that we would have to provide him with the money to cover the cost. Since he is well aware of this, for which he would never be blamed, he will never again take any chances in driving a car."

"What about his wife and children driving the car?"

"If any children are not citizens, they will be living in the world of free will and fall under the laws of their country. Once they become citizens, they assume responsibility for themselves. But as for a wife, she and her husband must become citizens at the same time, and until they both pass their examination, they are not citizens unless someone assumes responsibility for them. As for hospitalization insurance, it is all the same. When a citizen is displaced and needs our help, we assume all coverage."

"How does the guarantee affect their marriage?"

"All the laws that tried to bind them together will become obsolete, and they will become immediately divorced upon passing their examination, but they will be prevented from hurting each other by the most powerful laws in the universe — the basic principle Thou Shall Not Blame. They will be free to leave each other if they can do this after all advance blame has been removed, and they know they will never be blamed or criticized, no matter how much hurt is involved. If either or both have been committing adultery, this is their business, but when the ones who are hurt fully realize that it is within their power to prevent this hurt from continuing, now that the other half of the equation also understands the principles (as with Harry and Alice), all those striking a first blow will be given no choice but to stop — of their own free will.

Every divorced and single person who becomes a citizen will have their age and other information recorded in their IBM office for the purpose of bringing people interested in marriage together. Since this only means having sexual intercourse because they will never desire to leave each other once the principles are practiced, all widows, widowers, divorced, separated, and single people will be given every opportunity to meet each other. In other words, Charlie, you would have no trouble meeting a citizen with whom you could have a more passionate relationship than you had with Alice and never have to worry about her not staying with you or losing your standard of living."

"But how is it possible to relate all this to communism? And what about competition within and between nations? How do the guarantee and basic principle affect the relationship between seller and buyer, or lender and borrower? What about pollution, and will all forms of advance blame — this judging of what is right for others — come to an end? One thing more: isn't it true that communism already guarantees its people against going below their standard of living?"

"The only way Russia could guarantee its people their standard of living is when nothing is required for this from other nations. War is the consequence of trying to gain control of those countries that are needed by competitors for the same purpose — to maintain and improve a standard of living. However, by uniting all mankind in the guarantee and by introducing the basic principle, the conditions that cause a preference for war are permanently removed. You will see this for yourself as I proceed. As for your other questions, Charlie, let me get a cold glass of water, and I shall continue."

THE SECRET

CHAPTER TEN
THE DISPLACED

"Now, the very moment someone passes his examination and receives his identification card, his credit becomes unimpeachable, simply because we will guarantee it. But let me show you why. If he should get displaced, the amount of money needed to sustain his standard of living will never be stopped, which removes that justification. If he bites off more than he can chew, which I discussed once already, and fails to pay his creditors, they are justified in coming to us because we are the ones backing him up. However, when he knows that we will increase the cost of the guarantee because of what he did, without blaming him in any way, he will be unable to derive any satisfaction from such an act."

"But supposing he does it anyway?"

"We would be compelled to investigate the possibility that he is mentally ill. If such were the case and he needed treatment of some kind, we would withdraw his card until he was well, at which time he would have a deficit for money owed to his creditors that we would incur, as well as sustain his standard of living. But when each citizen understands thoroughly all the principles, they would never be able to find any satisfaction in biting off more than they can chew unless they are really mentally disturbed."

"Supposing he is not mentally ill. Let us imagine that some counterfeiter wishes to get out of his present line of work because he knows he could get caught and go to prison, becomes a citizen and receives a guarantee that was estimated at $300 a week. He then uses his IBM identification card to buy a big mansion, several cars, an airplane, and many other things on credit. He then borrows a million dollars from the bank, but when the very first payment for all these things is in default, his creditors go to his IBM office to collect their first installment. Seeing what he did, we call him in to test his mental balance and discover that he is not sick; what happens then?"

"Once we have ascertained that he is not mentally ill and that he deliberately wanted to hurt us, there is nothing we can do because we know that he couldn't help himself. We would continue paying his creditors, and if he used up his million dollars and still did not want to work for a living, he could steal more from us because we would never blame him for hurting us this way. But he knows that he doesn't have to hurt us this way unless he wants to, for over this he knows he has mathematical control, and when it fully dawns on him, when he passes his examination, that we would never hold him responsible for what he can never justify, he will completely abandon all such ideas — unless he is really mentally ill. However, just in case a mentally ill person did manage to pass his examination, he would still be prevented from buying on credit beyond his standard of living because his creditor would ask to see his identification card, and on it would be recorded the amount of his guarantee. If the purchase is too great, according to the judgment of the lender or seller (remember, the installments must come out of the guarantee, not out of his cash reserve), this transaction would be reported immediately to his IBM office. If he did not buy beyond his means but failed to pay his installments when due, we would pick up his condition soon enough. However, the odds of someone hurting us as a result of being mentally disturbed after becoming a citizen are so remote that it may never happen. As a consequence of this unimpeachable credit, the small lending companies, the installment houses, and everybody who is charging higher prices and rates of interest will be forced to come down or go out of business, which will give the consumer more spending money, increase production and employment, reduce the amount of money needed to sustain the guarantee, and therefore increase our spending money all the more. Instead of a vicious cycle, we will have a beneficent cycle, even though the credit investigation and collection agencies to service the accounts of citizens will be permanently displaced, as will lawyers. These people will be forced to spend or invest all their cash reserves before coming to us for help, but if they can't find a job or one that will make up the difference, we will supply it, so they have nothing to worry about. Also displaced in due time, because nobody will be spending their money in that direction, will be burglar alarms, locks, armored cars, vaults, safes, private and public eyes, floorwalkers, the banks as a place to safeguard money, guards, judges, jurors, the entire penal system, travelers checks, money orders, credit cards (all but the IBM), the

Commissioner of Motor Vehicles and his entire operation; the President, Vice President, governors, mayors, and all politicians that have been involved in blame of some sort. All the armed forces of the world, including the police, will be permanently displaced in due time, as will everything manufactured for war and crime. This will take place on a gradual basis as the citizens increase; however, the lawmakers will not be displaced because they serve a useful function. They will analyze every possibility of hurt that could exist and make it known. Whereas before we were controlled by the fear of punishment, which allowed those who thought they could beat the laws to attempt things without any regard to who got hurt, now we are prevented from desiring to disobey a just law because the fear of being excused for hurting others offers no satisfaction when all the principles are understood. If the lawmakers feel that the earth is overpopulated and pass a law (a recommendation) that two children per family are sufficient for our needs, this does not stop a husband and wife from having six if they want to, but when they know that this is a hurt to the economy for which there will be no blame, they will prefer staying within the limits recommended by the lawmakers. However, any couple that decides to have one or none would report this to their IBM office, and the difference could be made up by those who want more. No partiality could be shown; therefore, a method, such as a lottery, would have to be devised to determine which applicants would be chosen to increase their family."

"But what about the Catholic religion?"

THE SECRET

"It comes to an end along with all religion simply because the members of a congregation, realizing for the first time that God is everywhere, not just in churches and synagogues, and realizing further that all evil is coming to a permanent end, will prefer spending their money in a different direction. But the clergy will not be hurt because their standard of living is also guaranteed. In fact, once celibates have passed their examination, they can marry. God absolves them of their vows through his laws, which are now being revealed.

In our present world, many people are punished not because they hurt someone but because they violated a law. This, however, was necessary to prevent the possibility of being hurt at a future time. Radar traps were set to slow people down, who were also given tickets for parking in restricted areas, not because they were responsible for hurting someone then and there, but because it could hurt others. But when a citizen knows that he is not going to hurt anybody by going through a long red light, for example, because no cars are coming, then it is obvious that traffic lights have come into existence only to allow an even flow of traffic in a heavily traveled area; otherwise, a stop sign would be sufficient. When a sign says no parking or stopping between the hours of 4 and 6 p.m., this is designed to allow the increase in traffic to flow as smoothly as possible. To be delayed because someone has parked along the curb is an inconvenience for other drivers, but the citizen could never desire to do this because he knows he would never be blamed or criticized for it. But if it were possible for him to time his stop so that he would not delay traffic, then nobody would be hurt, whereas in our present world he could get a ticket for this anyway, as would happen if he went through a red light though no traffic was coming. This means that all the laws that are now in existence will remain because they are needed to control the noncitizens and will act as a guide to the citizens who are placed above them. A noncitizen moves away from libel because of the laws. A citizen will move away from it because he can't find satisfaction in hurting (or inconveniencing) anybody when he knows he will never be blamed."

"What happens to the people who knock at doors to make their living, solicit on the phone, etc.? This is really not an annoyance to those who buy, but it is to the ones who are weeded out in the process."

"All forms of advance blame are coming to an end. When a solicitor knocks at your door, rings your phone, or approaches you directly on the street to buy or donate, he is actually judging that you can afford what he is engaged in; therefore, he is striking the first blow. If you decide not to drop a coin in his can, to close the door, or to hang up the phone without listening to what he has to say, you are blamed. Consequently, all those who earn their living by contacting people directly will have to resort to some indirect method of advertising what they have (once they become citizens), simply because they will never be blamed for any punishment imposed as a means of getting what they want. In other words, knowing in advance that they are wrong, they will no longer be able to justify some form of retaliation by making it appear they are right. Even inside a store, the salespeople will wait for the potential buyer to make the first contact because he may just be looking around. This means that buyers will always travel to see the sellers, never the other way around, and advertising, which is an indirect medium of contacting potential buyers, will be used very heavily."

"But some companies cannot afford to advertise, that's why they pay out larger commissions. Besides, some products and services need long, drawn-out sales pitches to convince the customers to buy."

"We are not going to tell anybody how to advertise his products, but just in case he can't compete and is forced out of business, we will guarantee his standard of living. Furthermore, if someone receiving a guarantee of $132 per week for 40 hours took a new job that required him to put in longer hours to meet his guarantee, then anything over the 40 hours would be an additional income. For example, if he put in 50 hours to earn this $132 when he was receiving $3.30 an hour for 40 hours, then he is actually earning at this new job $2.64 an hour, or $105.60 for the week. Since his guarantee calls for $132 for a 40-hour week, he is still entitled to draw $26.40 from his IBM office because this is the amount by which he is still displaced. He would actually be earning for the week $158.40, but he put in ten hours overtime to do it."

"But knowing this, why should he desire to put in overtime when he might never be able to wipe out what he owes?"

"This is a decision for him to make if the particular job did not call for 50 hours. But if he was working 40 hours to earn his $132, he might not desire to put in overtime, which would again create more employment opportunities for others."

"What about all the litigation over contractors not living up to the terms of an agreement?"

"Everything will still be in black and white, so both parties to an agreement will be aware of the terms, but now, instead of a contractor trying to conceal anything, he makes absolutely sure that everything is revealed and thoroughly understood because he cannot find any satisfaction in not living up to what he promised, for which he would never be blamed. He would explain very carefully the differences in materials and their cost, but he would never have to worry about getting paid because if the customers want work to be done, they will borrow the money if it is available or arrange terms with the contractor."

"What about the censoring of films and the professional critic, aren't they engaged in blame?"

"They are, and both get displaced. There is no way that films or plays about sex can hurt citizens or cause them to hurt others. As for the critic, when he realizes that his criticism is a hurt for which he will never be blamed, he will desire, of his own free will (as will a person engaged in holding beauty contests), to change his job. The producers will advertise their show, and of those who see it, some will like it, others will not, but no criticism will be possible. If more people like it and consequently the producer makes a profit, this is his business; if fewer people like it and he loses, this is also his business.

Sports will continue because this is a source of entertainment for many, but the blame that exists between ball players and umpires will come to an end. An umpire is doing the best he can with the tools he has, but when he knows that the players will never criticize his decision because they know he can't help himself, he will do everything in his power to make absolutely certain he gives a correct call, and this will compel him to resort to slow-motion television pictures wherever possible. In fact, it is not too difficult to install a protected camera right behind the plate while the umpire sits in a box with a television that has been screened off for strikes and balls. When a bell rings, he yells, 'Strike.' As for pollution, once all blame is removed, every citizen becomes responsible for their own contribution towards this evil that affects the health of those whose bodies cannot take it. The person who drives a car will make sure that his exhaust has been reduced to its lowest point, as with all the other forms of personal pollution. The factories — not only because they are in competition and wish to find better ways of competing but also because they are not being blamed — will do everything humanly possible to correct this condition, which is a part of our standard of living. At the same time this is going on, science, those men and women who are searching for solutions to forms of hurt that affect all mankind equally, such as pollution, will let us know how much money is needed to cover the cost of research, and all of us who can afford to, will desire to contribute towards this on an equal basis. If 100 million dollars were needed and we had 2 billion citizens who could afford this from their cash reserve, then each one would contribute a nickel."

"For the life of me, I can't see how you are going to relate all this to communism, when their way of life is so different."

"Let me show you how by going inside the country where my father was born. Now you must understand that the guarantee and the IBM offices will be set up in Russia, as in all countries, and that the differences in purchasing power between nations in relation to labor will be evaluated so there will be perfect equality. In other words, if one dollar is needed from each citizen towards the guarantee, and if our dollar is worth more or less in world exchange, the difference would be rectified so that everybody contributes the same amount."

"But the communist citizen will not have any money as such. Russia is a huge army, and just as clothes and food are issued to soldiers, this is the way everything is distributed to the communists. How can you rectify this?"

"Simply by following our magic elixir and removing all forms of blame."

"But wouldn't that allow a great portion of the population to leave the country, like many of the Jews who can't wait to get out and go to Israel?"

"You must remember that once a communist becomes a citizen of the new world, he, like in the United States and elsewhere, will be placed above the laws of his country and be free to do anything he wants, provided he can do it without hurting anybody, for then he would be prevented by being denied any satisfaction. So, if his leaving (the loss of his job) hurts the economy in any way, although he is free to go, he would prefer to remain. Furthermore, his standard of living is guaranteed to never decrease as long as he loses his job involuntarily. If he quits voluntarily, even though nobody is hurt, his guarantee then becomes the basic standard of living. In other words, if someone has a guarantee of $130 and quits his job to take a new position paying much more, this is his business, provided nobody gets hurt; otherwise, he would not do it. But if he should lose this new job and need our help, his guarantee would be whatever the basic standard is to supply him with the necessaries of life."

"I understand, but wouldn't he need permission from both countries; that is, wouldn't he need to know that nobody would be hurt in either nation before feeling free to emigrate?"

"He certainly would, and in every nation there will be this group of lawmakers who will analyze every possibility of hurt that is not on the surface, and a part of these groups will do the same for the United Nations of the world.

Once the IBM offices have been set up in Russia (or any communist country) and someone becomes a citizen, he will go through a similar process with certain variations. The government accountants will record his gross income, which is the total number of hours he works. They will then figure out exactly what his standard of living is in relation to labor hours. If he works 40 hours and his standard of living (his clothing, food, shelter, medical care, entertainment, and all other personal services) is equal to 20 hours, then he is taxed 20 hours of his total labor time. Right at this point, a great change for the better is about to take place, and here is the primary difference between capitalism and communism.

In the United States, the government spends the tax dollars on anything it thinks is advisable, but how the profits are spent is left up to the people. But in Russia, the government not only decides how the taxes should be spent but also the profits, giving the people no say in this matter at all. Consequently, millions of Russians are compelled to remain at the lowest standard of living while someone else reaps the profit from their labor. But remember, this came about out of mathematical necessity, for which no one is to blame. Now once the standard of living is estimated in labor hours, the difference between that and his gross income (in our example, this would be 20 hours since 40 was estimated as his gross) would be broken down so it can be seen how much of these remaining 20 hours are being used towards sustaining the standard of living of others and how much is a surplus that is sold in foreign exchange. We shall assume that 10 hours is a surplus. But here we are faced with the same thing that confronted us in a capitalist nation. The new citizen observes that he is being taxed (putting in labor) to pay for services he derives no benefit from, and for the first time, since this is a judgment of what is right for him, he is going to invest his labor (these 10 hours) in another direction. Consequently, these displaced people (whoever they are) will have to supply their own labor time to sustain their standard of living. It is the same here. We are not going to spend our money in any direction that does not benefit us personally in some way, unless we want to. This means that the Russian citizen has just picked up 10 hours of profit — the labor that he is not going to pay any more in taxes that do not benefit him — although he will use these 10 hours of labor time to contribute towards the overall guarantee if it is needed, as was already explained. However, these displaced soldiers, police, and other government workers, as well as the manufacturers of war equipment, are completely free to get other employment, and if there was none available, then all the citizens in the world, not just those in Russia, would contribute an equal share of their labor or money to sustain them. The group of lawmakers in Russia will analyze the entire situation and discover that these displaced people can be put to work in various jobs, but each person will be allowed to select the kind of work he prefers, provided he can qualify, without any partiality being shown. If they were working 40 hours before getting displaced, this is the amount of time they would continue putting in."

"I don't understand how the guarantee works if all the displaced in Russia can find immediate employment. How is it possible for them to need our assistance?"

"If Russia needs to sell certain surplus products in order to maintain her standard of living, changing jobs does not affect this, but if she cannot supply the needs of her people (which includes everybody's standard of living), then we, those of us who can afford it without going below our own guarantee, would contribute an equal share so she could have the power to purchase what is needed from other nations, assuming that she has done everything in her power to sustain her own standard of living. In other words, before a millionaire can come to us for help, he must be broke, and if Russia has other surplus products that she planned to exchange for certain luxury items, she would have to use them first in the direction of maintaining her standard of living. Now let us return to our comrade, who is earning a gross income of 40 hours, twenty of which he is using to pay others to sustain his own standard of living, ten to supply the labor for those who give him nothing in return, and the remaining ten is the surplus that will be used in exchange for whatever is desired by the leaders. This means that if Russia reaps a profit for the year of 600 billion dollars and there exists a potential of 200 million citizens, then all those who are already citizens would receive an equitable distribution of the profits, not an equal distribution. Instead of receiving $3000 each, some might get $2500 while others receive less or more, but this would depend on the amount of labor time that each contributes towards the surplus, or, to express it differently, on what stock each person holds in this gigantic corporation. If our friend's 10 hours every week were worth $3000 at the end of the year, and if he only used up half of the ten hours he had available for the contribution to maintain the overall guarantee, then, at the end of the year, he would have picked up another 5 hours times 52 weeks, which would give him an additional profit of $1500, or a grand total of $4500 for the year. Naturally, if our IBM accounts were cleaned out, he would only have this $3000, and if we still needed money to finance the guarantee, his share would come out of his surplus profits, that is, if he didn't spend this profit periodically before the end of the year (in other words, after every exchange or sale). Remember, by spending it, he reduces the amount needed to sustain the guarantee because this creates the need for additional employment. By not spending it, it becomes a surplus that can be used to sustain those who can't find employment because it was not spent or exchanged. Now all that has to be done to satisfy every communist nation is to allow these profits to be spent in a manner that will benefit each individual, not just certain groups, and this is easily accomplished with the help of our lawmakers, those who search for what is and what is not a hurt. They will give priority to any improvement that benefits all the people equally, but once this has been set aside and they will not be able to take advantage, then the next priority will be what affects those in a prescribed area. If the total profits are not needed in either of these directions, then the individual can do what he wants with his own share. He could order things from other nations, invest it with other nations, even gamble with it, if he wants to. He can even buy what he could never get before, from his own country. In other words, if the displaced are used at jobs that increase the luxuries of the nation, whereas before the leaders distributed these at their discretion, the citizen who shows a profit can buy immediately, after a fair method of determining who goes first would be devised."

"But to gamble and buy from other nations, wouldn't this require that the labor hours be converted into dollars and cents, and wouldn't a medium of exchange have to be manufactured?"

"Labor can very easily be converted into dollars and cents, but a medium is not necessary when the purchaser can have the amount deducted from his IBM account while the seller has his credited. Far be it from me to tell the leaders of the Russian corporation how to run their business. I'm only replacing one set of laws with another, which gives them no choice as to what direction they must go for satisfaction."

"This whole thing is too fantastic, is all I can say. Your basic principle gives the appearance of being a panacea, although I don't think it can cure cancer, heart disease, and many of our medical problems."

"Perhaps not, but you are about to see another miracle performed that is related to the medical profession."

CHAPTER ELEVEN
THE WISDOM OF SOCRATES

Many years ago, Socrates was considered the wisest man of his time because he discovered that the primary difference between himself and others was that he knew he didn't know, whereas they didn't know either, although they thought they did. You reminded me of this the other day, Charlie, when I first told you about my claims. However, there is quite a difference between the knowledge resulting from the perception of mathematical (undeniable) relations and that which arises from syllogistic reasoning or observation. In other words, people who don't know the truth but think they do are projecting some kind of fallacious standard upon a screen of undeniable substance, and then because they see with direct perception — with their very eyes — what gives their knowledge the appearance of truth, they are convinced that they know whereof they speak. But what concerns me is not that they don't know they don't know, but the fact that they could hurt us by convincing us that they know when they really don't.

"Well, what is this other miracle?"

"Now refrain from jumping to conclusions, but three-quarters of the medical profession will be permanently displaced."

"You must be kidding! I just don't believe it! This is quite a surprise if true. But how can you make such a statement when this really depends on a reduction in those who need doctors? Are you going to make three-quarters of all sick people well? Is that what you mean? Or are you trying to tell us that they are not sick to begin with?"

"Neither. I don't have the knowledge to make sick people well, nor do I have the knowledge to know that they are not sick."

"Well, what are you talking about? We have a shortage of doctors as it is, and if sickness continues at the same rate, with only 25% of doctors to take care of everybody, we're in a bad way."

"The reason the medical profession will be reduced to such a degree is simply because our guarantee and basic principle are going to convince 75% of the doctors that they really don't know if they are doing what is best for their patients. And when this takes place, these doctors, who are citizens, will stop prescribing unless they are absolutely certain of what they are doing. You see, in the world of free will, definite conditions must exist for a doctor to open an office and practice his profession, but when these are removed in the new world, he is compelled to move in a different direction for needed satisfaction."

"This is me, Larry, not Charlie. Maybe he understands these general statements; I don't. Take me by the hand and show me exactly what you mean; is that asking too much?"

"It's like this, Jim. A doctor must always be in a position to shift his responsibility just in case something goes wrong and his patients get worse, and he must always be able to justify that what he prescribes for them will not make them worse. If he cannot meet these requirements, he will be forced out of business. However, you must understand that the great need to earn the money necessary to sustain his standard of living, which compelled him to justify anything the least bit questionable, is being removed by the guarantee. But let me draw up a comparison for better understanding. A salesman is able to justify telling white lies in order to earn a commission because he needs this money for his livelihood, but if the product he was selling could do serious harm to the buyer, then he would need a stronger justification; otherwise, he would be compelled to look for something else to sell. If he couldn't find it, then he would risk the consequences as the lesser of two evils unless, as in the new world, he is guaranteed his standard of living."

"I still don't understand. I guess I didn't go far enough in school."

"You will understand when I'm through. Now let me ask you this: What makes a doctor feel or know that he is qualified to heal the sick?"

"I would say it is the fact, at the very beginning, anyway, that he has received a diploma from a recognized university and a license from the government, which gives him the legal right to open an office and charge a fee to those who consult him."

"This is perfectly true. He knows that this right is not given to those who do not qualify — those who did not study for eight years and pass all the necessary requirements. Furthermore, there are all kinds of word relations that he can project to make himself feel all the more qualified, such as unqualified in relation to quacks and qualified in relation to doctors. Because some are quacks and therefore unqualified, they do not know whereof they speak. But he is a doctor, which means he is qualified; otherwise, he would never have been given this right to open an office; therefore, he does know whereof he speaks. How many times have you heard the expression: 'You do not know what you're talking about because you're not a doctor?' And how many times does a drug firm advertise the value of its products by relating them to the fact that even doctors recommend them, which is proof that there is no harm in their use? Doctors can't harm you; only quacks can, these unqualified charlatans, the pushers who sell their products without a prescription and tell you there is no real danger. Have you gotten the picture so far?"

"I can understand this, but this is not proof that they are not qualified."

"Let me make one thing very clear. This is not a criticism of the medical profession any more than my describing Hitler's slaughter of 6 million Jews is a criticism. Everything developed out of mathematical necessity, and that is exactly how everything will continue to develop. Furthermore, I am not trying to prove that doctors are not qualified because I do not have the knowledge to know this. I am only going to demonstrate that they will convince themselves of this when certain changes are compelled to come about. But when these doctors, of their own free will, stop prescribing, then they will know that they also don't know the truth, and this, nothing else, will put most of them out of business. Their next justification comes from the fact that there are malpractice laws, which means that if they conform to the Hippocratic oath and stay away from those things that could cost them their license, they are qualified to do everything allowed within their particular field. If some are general practitioners, they are allowed to prescribe any medicines that they think will help their patient. In most cases, he gets over his cold, cough, fever, or stomachache, and credits them with the cure."

"Are you implying that they were not responsible for making him well?"

"There are five possibilities of what could happen as a result of a doctor prescribing something or nothing. The first is that patients could die or get worse from their illness unless the doctor prescribes certain drugs or operations. The second is that they could die or get worse in spite of the treatment. The third is that they could die or get worse because of the treatment. The fourth is that they could get better in spite of the treatment. The fifth is that they could get better without any treatment. The first, second, and third possibilities are what doctors resort to for justification, but just in case something goes wrong and the patient gets worse or dies, they must be able to shift the responsibility away from themselves, and in that case, the second allows them to say, 'We did everything possible. If the patient had been brought to us sooner, we might have been able to save his life, his kidney, his leg, his eye, his lung, etc.' I am not implying that I know because I don't know when there are so many possibilities, but the patient believes the doctors know the truth, and because he does, he credits them with the cure. Because their patient invariably gets well in the majority of cases, sooner or later, and never seems to get worse as a result of their treatment, they derive renewed confidence in their qualifications to heal the sick. But whereas the general practitioners don't need too strong of a justification to prescribe drugs, surgeons do, because they are about to remove a part of the body. This justification is derived from three primary sources: One, if the operation is not performed, the patient will surely die. Two, even though they are not absolutely certain he will not die, the possibility exists, and since the removal of the particular part will not in itself endanger his life because it was already proven that man can live without these various parts of his body, especially when he has two of many things, they justify it on the grounds that it is the best procedure under the conditions. Last, they use Darwin's theory of evolution to justify the removal of vestigial organs even when there is no danger to the patient's life. They tell parents that the tonsils are more trouble than they are worth, as with the appendix, and the one sure way to prevent tonsillitis and appendicitis is to remove these useless organs that do us more harm than good. But just supposing Darwin is not right, and that these are not vestigial organs left over from the last mutation, what then? Then the surgeons would not be able to justify the removal of these organs unless the patient's life was in danger. The Jews justified circumcision on the grounds that it was a religious sacrifice ordered by God himself, but when many parents began to question the dangers of such an operation, and since man was becoming less and less religious, the medical profession was consulted for its opinion on removing the foreskin, and sure enough, it could be seen that not removing it was less healthy, which could be true. The fact that the baby was momentarily in pain and suffocated with wine was unimportant because this was done for his benefit. Besides, this piece of skin was also vestigial, something man was better off without."

"Have both of you followed me so far?"

"I'm sure Charlie has also, so continue."

"Now, in order to demonstrate why this great change is compelled to come about (God is giving us no choice), I shall resort to a personal experience in my life, and one in that of Will Durant.

About two and a half decades ago, a friend, 22 years old, was advised to have his tonsils removed, and died under the knife. The doctors involved did not break any malpractice laws, so they were not punished for this. Sometimes these things will happen, and that is why they make it very clear that they will do everything in their power to help you, but they can't guarantee anything. The risk may be very small, but this is the price you must pay if you want their services. Anyway, when the parents of this boy heard that their son had died during a tonsillectomy, they were overwhelmed with grief and accused the doctor of negligence. It certainly did not satisfy him to be accused of this, and he defended himself vehemently, blaming everything but himself. What actually caused my friend's death, I never did find out, but this is unimportant. My father also died in a hospital, and the doctors adduced the second possibility to satisfy their conscience.

"Durant, on the other hand, writes in his book Mansions of Philosophy: 'In the first three months we were guilty of a grave blunder, for we allowed our child to be used as a laboratory for a newfangled form of desiccated milk. It is a crime which many years of parental solicitude cannot quite clear from our memories. We realize now, with Benjamin Franklin, that the human race should beware of young doctors.' He blamed himself as well as the doctor, who blamed the manufacturer, who blamed his chemist, who blamed his assistant, who blamed the shipper, who blamed the farmer, who blamed somebody else. A chain reaction of blame ensues because nobody wants to assume responsibility. The surgeon blamed the anesthetist, who blamed the nurse, who blamed, and so on. Usually, when these things occur, they are hushed up, and since the doctors are never responsible, otherwise they could never practice, the possibility exists that they have been allowed to hurt others with impunity, as the expression goes. Now pay close attention to what happens when we imagine something that will not occur with doctors who are citizens of the new world, so we can see why it will not. The parents and siblings of my friend, who is undergoing a tonsillectomy, are waiting patiently in the other room for this minor operation to be over when the doctor walks in.

'Is everything all right, doctor?' the mother asks.

'I don't know how to break this to you any easier, but your son just died under the knife.'

THE SECRET

Upon hearing this, all four of them began to cry bitterly because this came as such a shock, but no one pointed the finger of blame at the doctor or his staff. They knew it was God's will that their son and brother die this way and that there was absolutely nothing the doctors could have done to prevent his death. But the doctors, for the very first time in their lives, know that it was not God's will that a person die this way because, over the desire to operate, they have mathematical control, and when it fully dawns on them that they will never be blamed for someone's death should this occur — even though it might have been their responsibility — they are compelled to advise an operation only if, by not operating, the patient will surely die."

"Are you saying that there will be no more operations in the new world except to prevent death or a more miserable life?"

"Can you think of any other way for a doctor to justify the possibility of making matters worse, when he knows that everybody must excuse him? This means that if he cannot see the mathematical (undeniable) relations that reveal a prognosis of death or of a life worse than death unless he operates immediately, he will be compelled to refrain from advocating an operation because he will never be able to blame anybody but himself should his patient get worse or die. Consequently, he is compelled to be absolutely honest with himself and his patients and become wise like Socrates, for when he is uncertain that an operation is the best course, he will simply tell them that he really doesn't know what is best."

"But this might not satisfy the patients who are in pain, or scared half to death. Besides, you have only spoken of operations. What about the administration of drugs to kill pain, get rid of colds and fevers, prevent lockjaw, rabies, and all the rest?"

"Let us first see what happens when new parents consult a doctor — who is a citizen of the new world — to find out what is best, to breast or bottle-feed a baby.

'Doctor, my wife's breasts are sore and tender, and she would like to know if you would prescribe some formula for our baby?'

'My friends, I honestly don't know what is better for this infant, a formula or mother's milk; consequently, I can't advise you. If you want me to make up some formula so you won't have to use your breasts, I will, but I can't say it is better or safer. Most babies do not have any problem, but I can't assume this responsibility to tell you that it is the better choice. This is a decision you will have to make all by yourselves.'

'Maybe I'd better stick with my breasts. Is there a charge for this?'

'None at all.'

"Now if this had been Durant and his wife, they would have been compelled to make their own decision. Since he would not dare to advise her because he certainly doesn't know; otherwise, he wouldn't have gone to the pediatrician in the first place, she is left completely alone to make this decision herself because these are her breasts. If she can find someone to prescribe a formula or wet nurse her baby, this is her business. But the fact that she still doesn't know this is better because to know she would have to have a tremendous amount of knowledge, she is afraid to go in the other direction and is given no choice as to what she believes is better for herself and her baby. Even though it is likely the baby would survive in either case, the possibility of cramps, indigestion, colic — call it what you will — which could be a headache to mom is also to be weighed. But whatever her choice, she must always move in the direction of greater satisfaction. Now you tell me; is this guy God a genius, or isn't he?"

"You are too much, Larry! But what about the administration of drugs?"

"When patients consult a doctor who has become a citizen, he will know that they are asking these questions even though they won't have to ask them:

'Doctor, I don't feel good and need you to do something for me, but are you absolutely positive that this medicine you're prescribing will not have any side effects and that it will not hurt me in any way? Are you absolutely certain that many years from now, should I continue to take these various drugs you always prescribe for my ills, I will not get cancer, heart disease, and many other things that have been plaguing our lives? I know that my allergy always clears up when you give me an injection, but is it possible that it would clear up without the needle, without the drugs, and if this is possible, why should I continue taking the needle and other things if you are uncertain of their distant effects on the body? Is it advisable to take aspirin, ibuprofen, and all the other pain relievers, or do these also have some distant effect on the body? Please, doctor, I am willing to pay heavily to know the truth, but don't take my money unless you really know what is better for my body.'

'My friend, the only thing I can tell you about drugs is what I do know. I know that aspirin and Tylenol can eliminate your headache, but I have no way of knowing what distant effects an accumulation of drugs can have on the cells of the body. I also don't know what is healthier: to use drugs to get rid of your aches and pains or to let the body correct itself. I don't know if, by not using drugs or by using them, your body will get worse. The most I can do is show you what immediate effects we know certain drugs to have, but I will not prescribe their use because I can't assume such responsibility. The drugstores have all of them, including heroin, LSD, and the whole shebang, and you don't need a prescription. The pharmacist won't advise you either as to what to use, but he will sell them to you if you want to buy them.'

'But doctor, you don't expect me to pay you for this visit, do you? You haven't prescribed one single thing for my ailment.'

'If I knew what was truly better for your body, I would definitely tell you, but since I don't, there is no charge.'

'Why did you bring up cancer? Are you implying that the use of drugs could possibly be the cause?'

'I really don't know, but the possibility exists. Wouldn't it be ironic if cancer disappeared along with this surplus of the medical profession?"

"I agree with him, Charlie. When these doctors become citizens, have their standard of living guaranteed, and know that they will never be blamed for any possibility of hurt done to a patient who must excuse what they can no longer justify, they will definitely be forced to think like never before, before prescribing anything, all but those who can guarantee results without the slightest possibility of making matters worse. But when will they be permitted to look for other work?"

"If a doctor's standard of living is $500 a week, and after using up all his cash reserve, his income starts to decrease because of a lack of patients, we will continue to supply the difference while he is a doctor, just as long as it is impossible for him to get a new job paying more than what his income has been reduced to. But if, for example, he can get a job paying $200 a week and his total receipts from his patients are now less than this, then he would be compelled to take the new job simply because the difference between this and the amount we have to pay him would cost us less."

"I can't stop saying what I said before. This whole thing is absolutely fantastic! Well, what's next, or shall we let Charlie carry the ball from here on?"

"That's not even funny anymore, Jim. One thing puzzles me, Larry. When most people consult a doctor, they are terribly afraid of what is going to happen if he doesn't prescribe something. The fact that he won't, wouldn't necessarily get rid of their fears."

"This is true, but God is forcing everybody to rely on their body to take care of 98% of all its problems by making all mankind realize that they don't know the truth about a tremendous number of these things, only thought they knew. If you are afraid of getting worse and wish to prescribe for yourself some drug, this is your business. On the other hand, if you are more afraid of the drug than leaving your body alone, this is also your business. But you have to decide this for yourself since the doctors who are citizens in the new world will be afraid to make it for you because the full realization that they might be responsible for making you worse, not better, who will never blame them, prevents them from offering excuses for what they can never justify."

"Are we to understand that a doctor in the new world will not be given a diploma and license?"

"This is correct. If he feels himself qualified to open an office and charge a fee, he will make this decision himself. Where citizens are concerned, there will be no such thing as legal or illegal. They will know what is and what is not a hurt, and they will never desire to hurt another."

"What about psychiatry? The doctors in this field, in a great many cases, do not prescribe operations, although they give drugs and shock treatments."

"A psychiatrist has been projecting onto this screen of undeniable substance, in a great many cases, a number of fallacious standards for determining the mental illness of people. The various words he uses circumscribe a behavior pattern which he then labels sick, just as certain differences in a person's facial features are symbolized as beautiful or ugly. Consequently, he easily justifies that innumerable people are mentally disturbed and in need of his help. Once he has identified all behavior patterns, it is then an easy matter to set up a course of treatment. However, possibilities exist here also that he could make matters worse by tampering with the mind, and unless he can guarantee results, which he might possibly be able to do, he will be compelled, of his own free will — especially when his standard of living will be guaranteed and when he knows he will never be blamed for hurting them just in the event he does — to admit to himself and his patients that he is uncertain of his knowledge. It is true that there are differences in behavior patterns and physiognomies, but certain words are not symbolic except for what we have projected from our realistic imagination. When someone does physical or other harm to another without justification, then we will know that he is mentally disturbed, but this is impossible in the new world. Until then, God is forcing us to leave the mind alone."

"What about the claims of the Cancer Society that cigarette smoking is a contributing factor in lung cancer?"

"I don't have the knowledge to agree or disagree, although I know one man in his nineties who has smoked two packs every day of his life, at least that's what I heard. I haven't examined his lungs so he may have cancer. I also know that smoking and drinking alcoholic beverages, as well as taking other drugs that have not been discussed here, will also come to a virtual end, but not because they are unhealthy diversions. I will explain why in a little while."

CHAPTER TWELVE
PARENTS AND CHILDREN

"It should be obvious that until children learn the principles and become full-fledged citizens, mother, not dad, will have to assume complete responsibility for everything they do."

"Why not him? I assume responsibility for my kids."

"Because he will not know any more than she will about raising children in the new world, nor will anybody else. Therefore, she would never have any reason to ask him questions whose answers she already knows. Should neither have undeniable knowledge as to what is best, as with breast or bottle feeding, mom will choose what appears to be better for herself and baby, as was explained."

"But isn't it possible that she could make all kinds of mistakes and hurt her children very much, having to depend on her limited knowledge?"

"She will be compelled to rely on her own judgment for all her decisions when no exact knowledge is available, but her judgment will be reinforced by the principles that she will desire to understand before having a baby. Your remark presupposes that other human beings possess greater knowledge, which could prevent these hypothetical mistakes, but in reality, once she understands all the principles, nothing else will be required to raise a healthy child. If she feels insecure even after learning the principles and decides to consult a psychologist or doctor, this is her business, and if he wishes to prescribe, this is his business, but before we assume this possibility, let us see what the new world has in store for her.

Now once she becomes a citizen and knows that not only her husband but no one else will ever criticize her for anything, which removes her desire to do what they thought was better for her in order to avoid the criticism, and when she also knows that her baby can never be criticized for anything because his will is also not free, she is given no choice but to prevent his desire from moving in the direction of those things for which blame was previously necessary. However, if she cannot prevent him from liking what she thinks is not for his benefit or from disliking what she believes is for his welfare (both without any form of blame), then she will know that the harm or benefit she perceives was only a figment of her imagination; otherwise, she could prevent it without blame."

"Are you saying that if she believes cake, candy, ice cream, cigarette smoking, marijuana, heroin, LSD, etc., are bad for his health and she cannot prevent him from liking these things without blame in any form, then she is to assume that they are perfectly all right to have?"

"But she can prevent him from liking these things without blame; that's just the point. It was only because of blame, he moved in the various directions that hurt himself.

THE SECRET

To understand this, however, let us observe a baby from the time of his birth.

In our present world, mom does not consider the baby's desires at all, only what she believes is better for him. Consequently, if he pushes away certain foods, she will blame his desire for not eating what she thinks he should, and will push the food right back in his mouth. She does the same if she feels he hasn't eaten enough. In her mind, there are certain standards that regulate or control her thinking. Carrots are good for the eyes; spinach will make him strong like POPEYE. If he doesn't eat enough (what she judges this to be), he will get underweight, undernourished, sick, and need a doctor. To prevent all this, she pushes him to do what he doesn't want to do. Now observe what change is compelled to come about when the principles are understood.

Since she knows that he cannot be blamed for disliking what she thinks he should eat, which is still her business, she is compelled to prepare and combine her food in such a manner that he will not reject what she wants him to eat. But if he does, there is nothing she can do because persuasion in any form, after he expresses his desire, is blame, which allows his taste and his body to determine what is better for himself. This means that all the values and standards she has been using to guide her decisions, provided she cannot accomplish them without blame in some form, must yield to his values and standards; but as a result, he will grow and develop like an animal. A mother cat doesn't set up a feeding and a bedtime, tell her kitten how much to eat or drink, nor does she give him baby cold medicine when his nose is running. By the same reasoning, once mom is compelled to move in a different direction, her baby's needs will also be controlled by what he desires. She will feed him not three or four times a day, but only when he cries to be fed. She will learn what meats, vegetables, and fruits he likes best and feed him only what he prefers. When he has had enough, he will let her know, and she will not blame him by insisting that he continue eating. This blame, from every indication, appears to be the cause of the mother's first problem, although I can't be positive. You see, when he is born, his stomach has never had any food at all, so it is possible that if mother's milk is not used since it developed with him, or even after he is weaned by pushing into it what he really doesn't want, he could get all kinds of cramps, indigestion, colic, etc. (I mentioned this once). Now if it should happen that he is going to be in pain, the only way he can express his feelings is by screaming or crying. Most parents have experienced this to a degree that was almost unbearable and at a time that was inconvenient. Either they were asleep for the night or making love. How many young mothers and fathers, not knowing what to do to stop this screaming, preferred to walk, rock, or bounce their child until the screaming stopped? This was not only an annoyance in itself, but right at this point is the origin of spoiling, which is a habit, not good or bad, they start and then blame him for. But when he is begging them to get rid of this pain in his stomach and they know of no other way to stop the screaming than to rock, walk, or bounce him around, what choice did they have? Before long, the pain subsides, and he falls asleep, but this wonderful feeling of being bounced around is remembered, and he knows that it occurs only when he screams at the top of his lungs. Soon, he screams, not because he's in pain but only to get mom and dad to give him that wonderful feeling again. However, when a mother is compelled to give him what he wants in the way of milk, it appears that the chances of colic are less likely to occur, and should he sleep soundly through the night, then the conditions that compelled them to select the lesser of two evils, that is, this rocking and bouncing to stop the screaming, never arise. Consequently, if she keeps him clean and feeds him the kind and quantity of food he desires when he's hungry, it is very unlikely they will be disturbed at all except when he needs to be changed and fed."

"But supposing this does not prevent the pain of colic, what then?"

"Most babies will grow and develop in spite of, not because of the kind of nourishment given, just as most people get well in spite of the drugs administered by the doctor because the body is capable of adjusting to most conditions. This is not a sufficient reason to feed the baby anything, but it is prevented primarily because the parents do not want to be disturbed unnecessarily, for this is a real headache. But should this pain occur after everything has been done to prevent it, they are compelled to select the lesser of two evils, and in the new world, this means letting the baby cry it out without this rocking and bouncing sensation because if they develop a spoiled child, then they will continue to have the screaming, which will make their lives miserable."

"Isn't it possible to spoil him in other ways?"

"Certainly, but you can easily prevent it from arising — if you want to — and you will want to when he can't be criticized for what he does. You must constantly remember that there are always two desires involved, and spoiling is a habit that requires your desire to satisfy the baby. Therefore, to prevent it, you must allow him to find his satisfaction without you, wherever possible, but if this denies you a certain amount of pleasure, then you must never give in to him when he insists that you continue doing what you do not want to. If by playing with him, both of you receive satisfaction, this is fine, but should you decide to stop and he makes a fuss, you have three possibilities: Never play with him at all, which is not satisfying to you. Continue to play with him, which is also not satisfying because you are choosing this only to put an end to his crying or screaming. Or just stop playing with him, regardless of the fuss he makes. Since the last possibility can never spoil your baby and will make him realize that he cannot control you with his crying, you are given no choice as to what is better for yourself when the facts are understood. In other words, whenever he tells you what he wants done, whether it is with screaming, crying, or yelling (unless it is to eat, sleep, or be changed), you must never give in because this allows him to use you for the satisfaction of his desire, which does not satisfy you. Once he sees that he can't control you, he won't make the effort and will never become spoiled. In our present world, parents blame him for not stopping what they started, and when he continues to make a fuss, they spank him, which starts a chain reaction of resentment."

THE SECRET

"I can understand all this, but something confuses me regarding blame. Mom has been pushing her baby to eat what he didn't want because she assumed she was right, which caused her to blame his desire; but when he begins to crawl or walk in the direction of furniture that could be broken, such as a lamp if he knocked it over, is she supposed to remove the lamp as she would a pin from the floor, stop him, or keep him out of the room altogether?"

"Let me see if I can answer Charlie's question. To say 'naw naw,' 'don't touch,' 'stop,' or just pick him up when about to knock over the lamp or put something in his mouth is a form of blame, and since we can't blame him for anything, it is obvious that we must put him in a playpen, play yard, or playroom so we can control the environment and prevent him from desiring to do those things for which it is necessary to blame. How was that?"

"Pretty good, eh, Larry?"

"Yes, except that it was completely wrong. What are we supposed to do when he gets older — put him in a playhouse, a play neighborhood, and then a play city? There is quite a difference between preventing him from breaking a lamp, which is hurtful to us, and preventing him from hurting himself. The purpose of putting him in a playpen is to control the environment so he doesn't hurt himself. Knowing that her husband would never blame her if the baby choked to death on a pin or a piece of glass, or hurt himself in any number of ways, she is compelled to be extremely careful about everything she does because it cannot satisfy her to be excused for carelessness that can no longer be justified."

"Wouldn't she be careful just to protect her baby?"

"This, too, but the other adds more weight. However, when he is allowed out of the playpen, we must prevent him from doing anything to hurt us, even if we have to blame his desire by saying, 'naw naw, mustn't touch,' etc."

"But wouldn't this encourage him to do more of what he is being blamed for? I know a kid who gets great satisfaction out of doing everything he is told not to do. 'Don't jump on the furniture!' He then uses it for a trampoline with his shoes on. 'You're blocking my view of the television.' He stretches out his arms, so you see still less. 'Put on your coat if you're going outside.' He takes off his shirt and shoes. 'Be careful not to spill that milk on the kitchen floor!' He walks into the living room and deliberately spills it on the new carpeting. I told two kids to be careful about splashing mud on my new car, and they said they would, but later, when I went outside, the fenders were literally coated with mud, and they were 4 and 5 years of age. It seems to me that no matter what you teach them, they desire to do the opposite. That's why I believe that if you stop the baby by blaming his desire to knock the lamp over, he will do it the first chance he gets. I've been compelled to punish my children; otherwise, I would have no control over them at all. How is it possible for me not to punish my son when he insists on doing what he was told over and over again not to do? Stopping him from breaking the lamp is teaching him that this is wrong, I grant that, but if he does it anyway, isn't it obvious that you have to punish him in some way? I thought that by controlling the environment, the baby would not be placed in a position to break the lamp, which would prevent the need to blame him."

"Sooner or later, he has to be taught what is right and wrong (this hurt to others), which means that he must be blamed and punished if this should occur. This is the principle of 'an eye for an eye and a tooth for a tooth.' However (and this is the source of the problem), there is no way he won't desire to strike back if he has already been hurt. His parents compel him to eat what he doesn't want, go to bed when he isn't sleepy, and punish him if he doesn't do these things. They pull his hair when combing it, which hurts, and frighten him when cutting it. Then, to top everything, they show tremendous partiality by calling other children cute, adorable, precious, smart, handsome, beautiful, etc. How long do you think it takes for him to know that he doesn't have what these words signify? By the time he is old enough to understand what is being said, he has built up such tremendous resentment towards his parents because they have hurt him so many times that he can't wait for an opportunity to strike back. Then, when he is told not to do something, the opportunity arises because he sees that he has control over something they want, and he will get tremendous satisfaction in opposing them, which starts a chain reaction of blame and punishment. However, this whole thing is prevented when we do nothing to hurt him, and this is prevented when they remove every bit of advance blame, this judging of what is right for him after he has already expressed his desire, assuming that his desire is not to hurt them, himself, or others. For example, if they decide to comb the hair of their daughter, who starts to cry, there is a conflict of desire, and if they ignore this cry and continue to comb, they are building up a resentment in her for this hurt. It is obvious that they're wrong because to satisfy them, which is to comb, she must sacrifice her own desire, which is for them to leave her alone. But under the conditions of being judged by friends and relatives for allowing their baby's hair to look so unkempt, they are given no choice but to choose the lesser of two evils. But when they know that this will not occur; that their friends will never criticize or compliment her appearance no matter how long, short, or twisted the strands of hair are, then they will get greater satisfaction in minding their own business, that is, in leaving her alone because this is what she prefers, and she is not hurting anybody with her preference. By constantly forcing her to do what she doesn't want with threats of punishment, which include asking favors (this was already explained), they build up this deep-seated resentment. This proves conclusively that the reason they were willing to hurt her was not because the condition of her hair was hurting them, but only because others were judging them by certain standards. In reality, what difference does it make if they decide not to comb her hair or let it grow to the ground, just so nobody judges them as inferior because of this? When this judging of what is right for others is removed, and it will be, then their baby will not be hurt and will not desire to strike back when they teach him the true differences between right and wrong, that is, what is and what is not a hurt to others and himself. Many children actually did things to hurt themselves as a reaction to getting back at mom and dad. By constantly offering dessert as a bribe to make them eat what they didn't want, they soon demanded it, or else they wouldn't eat. Fearing for their health, the kids were soon allowed to live on candy, cake, and ice cream because this was the only way some of them would consider eating other foods. No child would desire to go outside on a cold day without a coat unless he got greater satisfaction in opposing his parents, who have hurt him over and over again. Seeing that nobody is looking, he dashes out of the house half-naked to hurt them and ends up hurting himself. By removing all forms of blame from the time of birth, he could never desire to do anything to hurt himself or others."

"But what about smoking and drinking? Isn't it possible that these things could hurt him seriously if we permitted it?"

"Certainly, it is possible, but you not permitting them hasn't stopped it."

"Well, when I get married and have children, I am going to do everything in my power to get them to eat fruits, vegetables, meat, and poultry rather than candy, cake, ice cream, and other junk. I would like to see them drink milk instead of soda and highballs, and I hope they never get started with smoking and drugs."

"This is your business, but if some parents prefer the other, that is their business. However, when all blame is removed and the children are allowed to go in the direction they prefer, all these things will be virtually wiped from the face of the earth, in due time of course. Let me show you why this is compelled to come about.

If you feel like eating cake, candy, or ice cream after dinner or prefer a drink before, during, or after, along with a smoke, this is your business, but you must not judge what is right for your children by encouraging or discouraging these things, for this is advance blame. To tell them that drinking and smoking are for adults only arouses their desire to be like you, and the more they are blamed, the more they will desire what you don't want them to have. If you say these are bad for their health, they will have a feeling you are lying and will want to find out why. This would compel them to continue with something absolutely distasteful in order to find out what it is you like. Soon, they will feel like a big shot, like an adult. However, if they are left completely alone, they might desire to taste everything, and when they do, provided no comments are made, they will find certain things very distasteful. Try to make a baby smoke cigarettes and drink alcohol. This is equivalent to giving him Castor Oil. By the same reasoning, if various desserts are placed on the table after dinner, with no comments, and bearing in mind there is only so much they can eat, you will be amazed to learn how very little of this will be eaten. Where are they going to put it? But when they are made to believe that dessert is something special and when it is used as a bribe, then they will not eat other things to make room for the dessert. They are actually like animals, and just as a dog would never prefer cake, candy, and ice cream to meat and vegetables, neither will they unless preconditioned. If left alone, even if the dessert was placed on the table at the same time as other foods, they would never prefer it to meat, fish, vegetables, milk, or fruit."

"What about other influences, such as birthday parties, weddings, Bar Mitzvahs, etc.?"

THE SECRET

"We will always have parties because this is a lot of fun, but we won't have weddings or Bar Mitzvahs in the Golden Age. Remember, religion and the way we now get married are coming to an end. But whether we will need alcohol and marijuana, ice cream and cake to have this fun depends on whether our children in the new world will like it. Remember, the people who have been denying these things won't be around, and when the decision is left entirely up to an individual who will never be judged no matter what he does, he might decide against it, but this is his business."

"Parents make such a fuss over clothes; will this continue in the new world?"

"Of course not, Jim, because this fuss is a criticism of those who do not wear the kind of clothes to get these complimentary remarks. Clothes are used for three things: to keep warm, cool, and covered. The moment we use phrases like, 'What an adorable dress!', then we wear them to get compliments. But when it is remembered that this is an inverted form of blame, as is pretty to ugliness, we will be compelled, of our own free will, to stop using all words and expressions that blame others, directly or indirectly, simply because this is a hurt for which there will be no blame. Children would never have any reason to criticize or compliment each other's clothes. The differences that exist could never start an argument or even arouse envy because these items are not a pleasure in themselves, until... until the parents react favorably or unfavorably. However, the differences in toys can cause envy among very young children because they feel the other got something better. But when all blame is removed, Dad is prevented from giving a toy soldier to his son and a doll to his daughter if they are going to be playing together because this difference shows partiality, which is a form of blame. Consequently, he would be compelled to prefer giving the exact same toys in every detail or none at all, and at birthday parties, there might be no solution but to abandon the giving of gifts publicly. In the distribution of food, everything must be perfectly equal; otherwise, blame is present, so measuring devices might have to be used."

"What about teaching a child good manners, how to eat with a knife and fork, brush his teeth, tie his shoes, dress himself, and say thank you? What about the chores that mother assigns to him? Supposing he drops his spoon on a dirty carpet, couldn't I teach him to wash off the germs?"

"How do you know that whatever germs were picked up might not be beneficial? Why must they be bad germs? Since you don't know this, although you are permitted to believe what you want, you can't teach him that what you do not know is a fact. However, you can do your best to get him to imitate you. If he drops a utensil and you wish to wash it off while he watches, this is your business, but it is not your business to blame him if he should not do this. If he imitates you, this is his business, but if he doesn't, this is also his business. If you are worried and wish to spread a sterile sheet across the room every time he eats, this is your business, because this makes no demands on his desire. If you want to brush his teeth and wash his face because you feel this is better for him, this is your business, but if he complains, you must stop because this is his business. If you put him to bed, this is your business, but if he decides to get up, this is his business, and you can't blame him for his desire because nobody is being hurt, not even himself. I'll guarantee he will go to sleep when he's tired enough, although I shall discuss bedtime very shortly in relation to school. As for a chore, you can assign him something to do, for this is your business, but if he decides not to do it, this is his business. He will desire to learn how to dress himself, make his bed, tie his shoes, and thank others simply because he will see you doing what is in no way distasteful to imitate."

"What difference does it make to the parents when they are not going to be judged for this, and when nobody is hurt? If the mother wants to make his bed, this is her business. As for good manners, the best in the world is when we have learned to mind our own business, and God is giving us no choice."

CHAPTER THIRTEEN
DISRESPECT COMES TO AN END

"Did I understand you to say that all drugs will be legal for a citizen?"

"That's correct. He can do anything he wants without fear of being blamed. In fact, we won't even try to stop him from becoming a dope addict. And if he's so dissatisfied with life that he prefers suicide, this is also his business."

"Well, what's next on the program?"

"I'm going to put a permanent end (now don't jump to conclusions) to all education."

"But that's ridiculous!"

"I told you not to jump to conclusions. Does this mean you want to bet your 40 grand again?"

"Not a dime, but education is something of great value, so why should you want to get rid of it, or is this because you're a self-educated man?"

"Do you consider yourself more educated than Jim?"

"I certainly do."

"Do you, Jim, consider yourself less educated than Charlie?"

"I never went to college, but he is a Ph.D., so isn't it obvious who is more educated?"

"But you did graduate high school while I didn't, so does this mean that you are more educated than me — or is it I? Why are you hesitating?"

"Charlie already pointed out that you are a self-educated man. In other words, some people are able to acquire an education on their own through reading and studying, and you are one of those who accomplished this; therefore, as to who is more educated, I would place both of you over me and you over Charlie, although he might disagree."

"I don't, though. I consider Larry's education absolutely fantastic, and I place him above all the professors I know."

"Supposing I were to tell you that nobody on this planet is more or less educated than anybody else, would this disappoint you?"

"Are you telling us that this word is equivalent to beautiful, handsome, pretty, cute, etc.?"

"That's exactly right. I'm going to prove that everybody is equal in value, no better or worse, and the only reason we have never been able to see this equality is because of words like educated, cultured, good, etc., which projected stratified layers of value on word slides, through our eyes, into the external world. Seeing these differences in relation to substance, which cannot be denied — and believing the eyes are a sense organ that allowed these undeniable differences to strike the optic nerve for us to see them — we were given no choice but to say, 'Seeing is believing.' However, the very moment these fallacious words are removed, a miracle is performed because then it becomes mathematically impossible to judge anybody as inferior in value, and we are given no choice because our magic elixir denies us the satisfaction necessary to continue judging others as ugly, uneducated, stupid, uncultured, unrefined, or inferior in value when this is disrespect and a hurt for which there will be no blame. How is it possible for me to call Charlie educated, or more educated than you, without placing you in a position of inferiority? It is true he went to school longer than you, just as I read more books than both of you, but does this make me better or you worse? What makes the Catholics better than the Protestants, or vice versa? What makes a White man better than a Black? Why is a flat nose less attractive than a straight nose or crooked teeth than straight teeth? Why is Beethoven's music classical and better than the Beatles' rock and roll? Why do we judge those who read Shakespeare and attend the opera as cultured, while those who read comic books, westerns, and watch soap operas on television as uncultured? Words have fooled everybody, causing people to squeeze their teeth together, get nose jobs, and push their children in the direction of values that could not be denied by direct perception. Parents who never completed grammar or high school and never learned to read or write were made to feel as ignorant as possible. Consequently, they began pushing their child in the direction of acquiring this education so they would receive at least a vicarious degree of respect.

This formal system of learning allowed each child to measure his education, and when the top grade was reached, as in your case, Charlie, he felt very proud of himself. These professors and Ph.D.s were like gods among mankind, and from their height of success, they not only looked down with patronizing disdain but exacted from everybody a formal degree of respect by demanding that they be called 'doctor.' This word, when analyzed, means, 'I have more knowledge than anybody who has not attained the same height with myself,' and from this source began the complete development of our unconscious ignorance because this pride in their achievement, which was necessary in the world of free will, permitted them to pass along, from generation to generation, theories and opinions that were accepted as facts only because they were professors, which justified anything they wished to teach. They were really educated.

But Will Durant, who had also attained the same heights in this formal manner, resented their preemption of education because he passed far beyond in his mental development what these professors and college graduates could ever hope to attain by going to school, and he began to look down on them, just as Edward Gibbon did. It irked him to such a degree because he considered education as something a definite part of the real world that when Spencer defined it as the adjustment of the individual to the environment, which Durant firmly believed 'resulted in the conquest of our schools by mechanical and theoretical science to the comparative exclusion of such subjects as literature, history, philosophy, and art,' he retaliated by writing: 'I believe that it is through reading, rather than through high school and college, that we at last acquire a liberal education. Today we think a man is educated if he can read the newspapers morning, noon and night; but though our colleges turn out graduates like so many standardized

THE SECRET

Fords every year, there is a visible dearth of real culture in our life; we are a nation with a hundred thousand schools, and hardly a dozen educated men.' Is it any wonder he was so disliked by those he had excluded from this liberal education, namely, the college graduates? Is it any wonder he became so popular among those who realized, for the first time, that they didn't really have to go to school to acquire this great benefit called education? He believed that this formal schooling made its graduates into 'good office boys, good clerks, and good technicians, who, when their workday is over, devour the pictorial press and crowd into theatres that show them forever the same love scenes on the screen and the same anatomy on the stage.' How dare these people consider themselves educated just because they graduated college. He firmly believed that 'this mechanical and practical education produces partial, not total men, subordinating civilization to industry, biology to physics, taste and manners to wealth. Education should make a man complete; it should develop every creative power in him, and open his mind to all the enjoyable and instructive aspects of the world. A man who is heavy with millions, but to whom Beethoven or Corot or Hardy, or the glow of the autumn woods in the setting sun, is only sound and color signifying nothing, is merely the raw material of a man; half the world is closed to the blurred windows of his spirit. An education that is purely scientific makes a mere tool of its product; it leaves him a stranger to beauty, and gives him powers that are divorced from wisdom. It is well that Latin and Greek are passing from our colleges, for they consumed a hundred times more effort than they were worth. As Heine said: 'The Romans could not have had much time left to conquer the world if they had first had to learn Latin.' But though the languages of Greece and Rome are necessary only to philologists, the literature of these nations is almost indispensable to education. A man can conceivably ignore Virgil and Horace, Lucretius and Cicero, Tacitus and Marcus Aurelius, and still become mature; but of all possible instruments of education that I know, none is so fine and sure as a study of Greek life in all the varied scope of its democracy and imperialism, its oratory and drama, its poetry and history, its architecture and sculpture, its science and philosophy. Let a student absorb the life and letters of the Periclean age, the Renaissance and the Enlightenment, and he will have a better education than any college can give him.' And then he arrives at the very heart of his definition.

'Education does not mean that we have become certified experts in business, or mining, or botany, or journalism, or epistemology; it means that through the absorption of the moral, intellectual and esthetic inheritance of our race we have come to understand and control ourselves as well as the external world; that we have chosen the best as our associates both in spirit and in the flesh; that we have learned to add courtesy to culture, wisdom to knowledge, and forgiveness to understanding. When will our colleges produce such men?'"

"What was your purpose in such a lengthy quotation?"

"I'm going to return to it later to reveal how the truth has been hidden behind a facade of ostensible words, but to help me accomplish this, let us first find out what our basic principle has to say about disrespect, because it appears that we are slightly confused as to who is showing this.

Today, if you do not remove your hat in the home of a person who expects this, he says, 'Would you please show us some respect and remove your hat?' In other words, in order to satisfy his desire, which is for you to remove your hat, it is necessary that you sacrifice your desire, which is to keep it on. This has been explained already, but it needs repeating. Since you are really not hurting him in any way, although this was a custom he believed was right, and since there is nothing he can do to make you take it off, because he knows that you would never blame him for any hurt that he does (and especially since he knows, after becoming a citizen, that he is wrong), he is given no choice but to respect your desire. However, if your hat was blocking his view in a theater, you would desire to take it off because the realization that this is a hurt to him, who would never blame you for this, removes any satisfaction in keeping it on. In other words, everybody who judges what is right for someone else is wrong and showing disrespect, and this knowledge puts a permanent end to all customs, conventions, etc., unless an individual prefers continuing with those habits that do not judge others. This means that all titles of respect, notwithstanding, are disrespectful because they judge what is right for others. If it gives you satisfaction to call someone 'Sir, Doctor, Professor, Mommy, Daddy, Uncle, Aunt, Mr., Mrs., Miss,' etc., this is your business because nobody is being hurt, but by the same reasoning, if you prefer to call him by his first, middle, or last name, this is also your business because he is not being hurt. But when you correct a child for not using 'mommy, daddy, uncle, aunt,' because this is a sign of disrespect, you are the one being disrespectful because, in order to satisfy your desire, it is necessary for him to sacrifice his. This doesn't stop you from teaching him to use 'mommy' if you prefer. However, should he hear someone calling you by your first name and he does the same, to correct this blames him, which means you are in the wrong. You see, God is going to prove that nobody is worse than anybody else, and therefore entitled to respect, but when these names are exacted, there is inequality and disrespect. Have I made myself clear?"

"You certainly have. I think a six-year-old could understand this."

"Now the greatest disrespect in the world is shown by parents to children, by teachers to students, and by all those who consider themselves intellectually superior, more intelligent, and more educated, to those who are judged inferior, less intelligent, and less educated. But how do we get rid of it? The answer is very simple when we continue to follow our magic elixir.

As was explained before, parents have a perfect right to judge what they think a child should eat or learn, but once the child has expressed his desire, even if it does not agree with theirs, he must not be blamed because his will is not free. Consequently, if they want him to learn reading, writing, and arithmetic, they must arouse his desire to move in that direction, but this is a very easy thing to do, and when they feel this has been accomplished, they will ask, 'Would you like to go to school and learn how to read and write?' But if for any reason he doesn't want to go, they cannot criticize him... unless they want to do what they know is wrong. This, nothing else, will determine when he starts school — his desire to go. Once his mind has been made up, he will be given an alarm clock and shown how to use it, for he will assume complete responsibility for himself even at this early age. But the problem that existed in our present life, which caused him to dislike what parents found of vital importance, will not exist in the new world; consequently, he will desire so strongly to go to school that every day, when the alarm goes off, he will be anxious, not reluctant, to get there. Let me show you why.

Since it is a form of advance blame to ask questions, the answers of which are already known to the one asking, the relationship between a teacher and his students becomes equivalent to that of a seller and his buyers. They are there to buy what they want to learn, not what he wants to teach, and he is there to sell this knowledge. This means that they can never ask him any questions if they already know the answer, because this is done only to find out if he knows what they think he should, and a judgment of what is right for him. The only person this concerns while going to school is him — no one else — but because of this apparently simple change, observe what takes place."

"Who does it concern after he is out of school?"

"The person who hires him for something. If an employer has several applicants for a job and only needs one, he has a right to test them to see who knows more about the work to be done. But knowing that the employer would never blame them for making mistakes and hurting him, they are compelled to prepare themselves so that if they are hired, they will never do anything to hurt him.

Children will be told by their parents that if they come late to school, this would be a hurt to the teachers who are trying to do their work without any unnecessary interruptions. They will also make them understand that even though this would be a hurt, there would be no criticism and no blame because everybody would know that he couldn't help himself. In other words, this basic principle is something parents and teachers will go out of their way to teach because it is the key to this new world. But once it is understood, it will bring about a marvelous change, even where bedtime is involved. Observe a comparison.

Durant writes: 'Many a bribe of tender words, and dimpled arms about the neck, has been offered us for permission to "stay up" beyond the year's decreed retiring time. But here we have been quietly and inconspicuously resolute; we will not condescend even to discuss so absurd a proposal; we turn it aside as a criminal idea, and send Ethel up to Morpheus every evening at her usual early hour. Now, though she is a great lady of almost ten years, she still disappears regularly at eight-fifteen, wishes us from the staircase "tight sleep and pleasant dreams," and is all tucked in and set by half past eight. The law has been broken now and then, as when some genius of the piano was honoring our home; but for the most part it has been with us a sacred monastic rule, a trifle of surpassing moment in our philosophy.' As you can see, he showed absolutely no respect for her desire to stay up beyond a time that he judged was right for her, but this was necessary under the conditions.

However, when the conditions change, a child will know that he has to be in school by a certain time; otherwise, this would be an annoyance to the teachers who do not want to be disturbed with interruptions when the class is started. Therefore, he would make sure his alarm clock is set to give him ample time. He knows he can't depend on his parents waking him, because this blames them should they not, and he also knows they will never insist that he go to school, because this blames him should he not. Consequently, he realizes that the responsibility of going or not going is entirely his business, and if he wants to be rested each day, he will have to regulate his own time according to what he feels he needs. Then, should some 'genius of the piano honor his home,' he might prefer excusing himself, since the guest was more a friend of his parents, rather than stay up late and be tired the next day."

"But supposing he does go to bed late and is tired the next day, what is to stop him from turning off the alarm and going back to sleep? When he awakens hours later, knowing that it would be an annoyance to the teachers to come late — who would never blame him for this — he decides to stay home for the entire day. How is he going to learn anything that way?"

"Your reasoning is filled with assumptions. You are assuming there will be something in school to make him not want to go, and you are also assuming that he will not learn what he wants to learn unless you push him. But when he is never made to feel the slightest bit inferior to any other child, and never hurt in other ways, his desire to learn will become insatiable.

The teacher will have a lesson, and when it is over, the pupils will be told that if they are interested in reviewing what they were taught, they will be permitted to take this same lesson home with them. He will never ask any child a question, the answer of which he already knows. Consequently, the burden of his inadequacy as a teacher cannot be shifted to them, and when he asks, 'Is there anything anybody doesn't understand?' he may be swamped with questions to reveal his own inadequacy. Since he cannot criticize them, and since this puts him to a great deal of work explaining simple things again and again, he will begin to instruct them in such a manner that everybody will understand. Today, children are afraid to let a teacher know they don't understand because he blames them for their lack of ability, and when others hear and see this, they also laugh. But when there are no comments, the children will not hesitate to ask questions if certain things are not understood. When all the distaste is taken out of learning, they will be extremely anxious to go to school. As soon as they are taught to read, another great change must come about.

The teacher is in the habit of testing children to see if they are grasping what he feels they should know, and the written test has become a part of the school system, just like graduation, report cards, and homework assigned by him. But since it is not his business to question them about things he already knows, here's what he says to them when a lesson is completed. 'Children, on my desk is a written test with the answers. If any of you are interested in testing yourself to see if you have learned everything, you may take this home with you. However, if there is anything you don't understand, you may come to me after class, and I will help you.' There will be no graduations because this criticizes those who do not graduate, no report cards to report to anybody, and no homework. Once criticism has been removed, these things have absolutely no value. When they feel ready for lesson number two, three, or four, or when they are ready to transition from grammar to junior high or from junior high to high school, they will announce this to those who need to know. They will have the opportunity to engage in competitive activities if they wish to, but under no circumstances will they ever be blamed if they don't want to or if they decide to discontinue something they were doing, as this is their business. Once they have been taught to read, the teacher will tell them about various books he feels they would understand, but whether they will desire to read is their business. He will also tell them about the various things they can learn at their next school, if they are interested, and they, not the teachers or parents, will select their course of study. They will be going to school not to get an education, to acquire culture, to get a degree, or to gain more respect, but simply to learn what interests them. If they want to study Algebra, Geometry, Trigonometry, and all the higher forms of mathematics, or Latin, Greek, History, Geography, the Periclean Age, the Renaissance, the Enlightenment, and everything Durant recommended, this will be their business, and if someone else does not desire these things, this is his business. Neither will be judged of greater or lesser value by words that stratify them. But here is where a tremendous change occurs because it takes hard work to do what some students have been doing to get their degree. Once the diploma is removed, along with everything else that was used to make someone feel superior, he will be equivalent to a man who was shipwrecked on an island after spending many years lifting heavy weights to develop huge muscles for others to see, unless he found pleasure in these heavy studies (in lifting heavy weights) or unless his great effort was for the purpose of earning a better living or becoming famous for something. Today we ask: 'From what university did you graduate? Did you complete high school? What kind of degree did you get? How far did you go with your education? Can you work out this problem? Do you know when Columbus discovered America? Can you name all the capitals and states in the Union? Do you read Shakespeare? Do you like opera, Beethoven, Corot, or Hardy?' Every question is designed to lower someone and raise oneself. But when this becomes mathematically impossible to do, then man is given no choice but to relinquish all those pursuits that had no other value. What good is memorizing the encyclopedia when no one will ask you the questions that he can get answered at the library or from his own set of books, unless you are going to perform on some show? And how are you going to ask them the kinds of questions that you would like to be asked when you already know the answer? Of what value is this information when you can't use it? If you wish to read ten thousand books, this is your business, but the only difference between you and those who only read three is 9997. But when you are allowed to use words like educated, cultured, and mature, then it is possible to convince yourself that the effort was worth it because you are now a highly educated individual, an intellectual. When these words are removed — and they will be (God is giving us no choice, as I have repeated) — then what each man prefers to learn or do is his particular education, and the word under these conditions loses all significance.

I found great pleasure in reading the books Durant recommended, but especially in studying his own Story of Civilization. This did not give me a liberal or any kind of education because there is no such thing, but it helped me to see things from a better perspective. It did not make me mature, cultured, or anything else, but it helped me accomplish my purpose. If it had not been for Will Durant, this book would never have been written. However, I am going to show you something very humorous as I paraphrase his definition of education.

In the new world, 'we are able to control and understand ourselves as well as the external world,' not because we have absorbed the 'moral, intellectual and esthetic inheritance of our race,' but only because we know what it means that our eyes are not a sense organ and that our will is not free. 'We have chosen the best as our associates both in spirit and in the flesh,' only because the knowledge that we will never be criticized, ridiculed, blamed, or punished in any way, no matter what we do, allows us, for the very first time, to select what is truly best for ourselves, even though we may prefer the Beatles to Beethoven, Zane Grey to Shakespeare, Elvis Presley to Caruso, the atmosphere of a poolroom to the 'glow of the autumn woods in the setting sun,' or a laborer as a friend to an author, philosopher, historian, or piano virtuoso. 'We have learned to add courtesy to culture, and wisdom to knowledge,' only because we have really learned to mind our own business, learned what respect is, learned that all mankind are perfectly equal in value, and learned how unconsciously ignorant of the truth we have always been, which wisdom makes it impossible to be discourteous when there is no culture, no education, and no other such knowledge to make us feel inferior. And we have added 'forgiveness to understanding' only because we know at last that man is truly not to blame, which gives us the understanding to prevent from coming back into existence that for which forgiveness was previously necessary. When will our colleges produce such men? Only when each person passes his examination and becomes a citizen of the new world."

THE SECRET

PART FIVE
IMMORTALITY
CHAPTER FOURTEEN — THE THIRD
SCIENTIFIC DISCOVERY

CHAPTER FOURTEEN
THE THIRD SCIENTIFIC DISCOVERY

"Don't tell me the long-awaited moment has finally arrived, and you're now going to put the icing on the cake. If my memory hasn't failed me, you said you would reveal something about death in a mathematical manner that will make everybody very happy, correct?"

"That is so, Charlie, provided they can understand the relations."

"Is it more difficult than two plus two equals four, and will it have anything to do with a spiritual world of souls?"

"Nothing at all, although two times two might be more difficult than addition for some people."

"I just can't believe it is possible to reveal anything after death. I know there are all kinds of beliefs, but for you to say your proof will be completely mathematical is somewhat ridiculous, I think; don't you, Jim?"

"I don't know what to think anymore. I take for granted; however, you will not be able to use the basic principle, is that correct?"

"Although it has been an infallible guide and miraculous catalyst through the labyrinths of human relations, it cannot assist me here; but it did not help other scientists discover atomic energy, nor was it used to reveal itself. That of which it is composed, this perception of undeniable relations that escapes the average eye, will take us by the hand and demonstrate, in a manner no one will be able to deny once it is understood, that there is absolutely nothing to fear in death, not only because it is impossible for us to regret it, but primarily because — now don't jump to conclusions when you hear what I'm about to say — we will be born again and again and again."

"No wonder you checked me, but this is similar to the belief in reincarnation."

"It has nothing to do with that or any other belief, nor does it mean anything else you might be thinking, because the life you live and are conscious of right now has no relation whatsoever to you in another life."

"This is quite surprising. You just said that I would be born again and again and again, and now you say there will be no connection between me now and me then."

"I realize that, but to help me explain it, I shall begin by asking a very important question. Doesn't it seem strange that of all the millions of years the earth has been in existence, you, of all people, should be born at this time to see the wonders of the world and the Inception of the Golden Age? Why weren't you born back in the time of Socrates, or why shouldn't you be born later after the transition has been completed?"

"I was born now because my father met my mother, fell in love, and got married. They gave birth to four children, and I am the third."

THE SECRET

"This is all very true, but it doesn't reveal a deeper truth. Does matter itself reveal atomic energy? Do the individual planets, moon, and sun reveal the solar system, unless you investigate this deeply? Do individual people reveal the mankind system? Does all of it together reveal the reality of God unless certain mathematical relations are perceived? Certainly, your mother and father mated and gave birth to four children, but this tells us nothing about the laws it is necessary to understand to know why there is nothing to fear in death and why we will be born again and again and again. At one time we were afraid of thunder and lightning, thinking it was the wrath of God, but now we don't fear the thunder and try to protect ourselves against the lightning. Until man discovered the cause of an eclipse, he was afraid that something terrible was going to happen, and it became an ominous sign that was blamed for whatever evil followed."

"I agree that my answer was rather superficial, but this is the only thing undeniable that I can see about that relation. I also agree it does seem rather strange that I was born now with all these millions of years the earth has been in existence. But strange as it seems, it really means nothing to me and doesn't stop me from having a horrible fear of death."

"Now the actual reason it is not strange that I was born now after all these millions of years, is because I, no one else, that is, not only I as I now am, but me as someone else, will always be conscious as long as mankind exists; and I shall prove this in a mathematical, undeniable manner."

"You can't be serious! How is this mathematically possible?"

"Would you like to bet your 40 grand again?"

"Never mind, but I still think it's impossible... with reservations, that is, after your blueprint performance. Well, show us; seeing is believing."

"The first step is to establish certain undeniable facts. So tell me, is there such a thing as the past? Does this word symbolize something that is a part of the real world?"

"Of course. Yesterday was Thursday, and there isn't any person alive who will disagree."

"I, too, will agree with that, but this does not prove whether the word past is an accurate symbol. Can you take it the same way you can with the words apple and pear, or two plus two equals four, and hang it up on something so I can look through it at the real McCoy?"

"You know that's impossible to do, so why do you ask?"

"In order for me to prove what seems impossible, it is absolutely necessary that I de-confuse your mind so we can communicate with each other. Now, the reason man cannot do what I asked is simply because there is no such thing as the past. All we have, in reality, is the present. A second ago, yesterday, last week, last month, two thousand years ago, are word slides in our brain projector through which we remember our experiences, that is, recall to our attention something that happened in our lives, but if we were not able to remember (store away these word slides that contain every conceivable kind of relation), the word past would never have come into existence because we are born, grow old, and die... all in the present. Everything that you can possibly do, from the time you get up to the time you go to bed, and even your sleep, is done in the present, as is the shining of the sun. Are we in agreement?"

"I understand and agree. Do you, Jim?"

"Yes, I do."

"The next fact to be established, and the most important, is to realize that it is mathematically impossible to see this world through any consciousness but your own. It is your eyes through which your brain looks out, not those of someone else."

"But others are conscious too, correct?"

"That's true, but their existence is seen through your consciousness. Now supposing we let A represent all the sperm and B all the ova pertaining to mankind, while the combination of one with the other will be designated C, which is you, your potential consciousness of existence. Let us further imagine that your mother and father want you, and as a result of mating, A joins up with B, but during their uterine journey, you, C, end up a miscarriage, which means that you just died. Consequently, you are not conscious of your existence because your body was never born to give you this. But your mother and father still want you, their first baby, so they try again, but this time you are born only to die one month later of a heart attack after taking a good look at your father. But still persistent and having a lot of fun, they try again with viable success, but 15 years later, you end up in a hospital where you die. Much older now, but still capable of propagating, and because they were not satisfied to lose you, they try again to bring you into existence. Now in actual reality, though hereditary differences exist between the three C's, the word you is a designation only for the viable substance that comes into the world and is identified with a name to establish these differences, which mom and dad grow to love. But what is the difference between the potential you who died during the uterine journey, the you who died one month after birth, or the you who died 15 years later? Because you are conscious of your existence and individuality during those years in the present, write a book, build a home, make a lot of friends who cry when you die, doesn't take away from the fact that you are a combination of A and B, which continues in existence even while you are alive and regardless of what happens to C. If you had died a hundred thousand times in the uterus of somebody, eventually you, which is a word to describe the consciousness of differences about yourself and the fulfillment of your parents' desire, would have been born. Consequently, the consciousness of your individuality, without understanding that you are not only C, which represents the hereditary differences that die, but A and B, which never die because they are carried along from generation to generation and, when united, develop into any C, makes you perceive an improper relation. Just because the entelechy of A and B develops into the consciousness of C, which permits the recognition of individuality, doesn't negate the substance from which C is derived. Even if all the individual characteristics lie potential in the germplasm, this still has nothing to do with consciousness, which is not an individual characteristic like your face. The word I or you not only reveals this individual difference between yourself and others, but your consciousness of this."

THE SECRET

"I'm failing to register your analysis. In your Yiddish lexicon, Larry, you farmisht my kop.

"I have him, Jim. Assuming that everything you said is true, who is born when mom and dad have a second child? If Oscar was the first, and he is now conscious of his existence, who is the second child born, not Oscar again, is that right?"

"You are right, and we have just arrived at the second half of the equation. Now, let us imagine that our parents, Adam and Eve, gave birth to ten children. You, me, Harold, Monroe, Ida, Roberta, Sue..."

"Is that the boy named Sue?"

"Don't be funny; one boy named Sue is enough. Also, Linda, Janis, and Madeline. Through the course of nature, these children, not knowing anything about incest, got married. Ida with Harold, me with Madeline, Monroe with Roberta, you with Janis..."

"But that only leaves Sue and Linda."

"Then Sue must be the boy named Sue. Anyway, in the course of time, these ten gave birth to 40 more children, and these to another 150 until the earth's population was all of 202. But Adam by now was a very old man about to die, and just before passing away, he said to me, 'Larry, isn't it strange that with all the years the earth has been in existence, I am alive, conscious right now of this world? I am conscious of you, my wife, your brothers and sisters, and all the rest of my family. When the last baby was born on my 100th birthday, I said to myself, 'Wouldn't it be wonderful if that was me, starting my life all over again so that I could enjoy the sun, stars, and all the other things for another 100 years?' But I knew this baby could not be me because this is me talking to you, and number 202 is a tiny infant, while I am worn out with age. It would be wonderful, though, if people didn't have to die, not that I really mind under the conditions because I've long since lost the desire to make love; but if I could be born again with a completely new body, it would be heaven on earth, and maybe in my new life there would be something to cover my feet so they don't get all cut up from walking on small pieces of broken stone.'

"Now pay close attention, because Adam's wish is about to come true, but it is important to understand that just as long as he is alive, any person born cannot possibly be him. However, when he dies, this body, this bubble of consciousness is gone, which makes it impossible for him to have any relation with the next child born or those still living. His family is not 202 after his death, but 201. Now answer me very carefully. If you admit that it is mathematically impossible to see this universe through any consciousness but your own and that you can only live in the present because there is no such thing as the past, who will possess this next bubble of consciousness when you die, assuming that you are Adam now and are no longer here?"

"It certainly could not be me. If the new baby is a boy, he will possess it. If a girl, she will."

"But how is it possible for you to say this, Charlie, when you are no longer here to say it? For this relation, he or she must pass through your consciousness, and you are no longer alive, so whose bubble of consciousness are we talking about? In other words, if it is mathematically impossible for you to say 'his or her' regarding this infant that was just delivered, because this must have reference to your consciousness, and your consciousness isn't here because you just died; and since the other 201 people in your family have their own lives but still want you, number 202, the next infant born is not 203 but you, who will grow, develop, and become conscious of your existence. Remember, the conditions are exactly the same before you are conceived and after your death. Since you cannot see this universe through the consciousness of another, when you die, what consciousness exists belongs to all those living. However, since you are no longer conscious of your existence when dead, and since it is mathematically impossible to see this world through the consciousness of another, and since everybody who is still alive has their own consciousness, it is obvious that the next person conceived and born after your death is not him or her — because this can only be in relation to your consciousness, which is not here anymore since you died — but you 202, not the person who just died, but an individual who grows, develops, and becomes conscious of his existence and individuality. Consequently, since there is no such thing as the past, and consciousness can only be your consciousness, which must exist in the present, your consciousness will always be here during every moment of time. This means that right after your death, you become the potential of any A and B combination into C, or, to express it differently, you become the fulfillment of your parents' desire to have you."

"I'm beginning to see the relation, but I'll have to go over it several times. How about you, Jim?"

"Vaguely, but I'm getting there. Even if I don't understand it completely, I'm still going to believe that he's one hundred percent right."

"If you examine all the facts, you will find them undeniable. This I or ego that you feel is definitely a reality, for it is you, no one else, that tastes, touches, smells, hears, and sees. But this consciousness is not only an individual thing like the various differences about yourself, which we have considered C, but also A and B, the potential consciousness that exists in the germinal substance. Since this substance is that from which your ego, the feel of yourself as an individual, is composed, and since this I or ego is also the conscious expression of this germinal substance, both are one and the same. Consequently, the consciousness of all mankind is the ego, or I, of the germinal substance that imparts individuality upon the birth of a child, as a tree does to a leaf in the spring of the year. But this all-pervasive consciousness, which exists always in the present (and here is the mathematical solution again), can only be your consciousness because it is mathematically impossible to see this universe through any consciousness but your own. In other words, you must be on the inside, looking out. It is this that enables us to say whether a million years ago or a million years hence, 'Isn't it strange that I was born now to see the wonders of this amazing world?' Consequently, death is a mirage to those who die and a reality only to the living, and it is our ability to recognize these deeper relations that gives us our knowledge of immortality and our freedom from the fear of death."

"I just got it, Jim! He's one hundred percent right!"

"I just got it too, and it's a wonderful feeling!"

"Soon it will dawn on you, as you more fully understand these relations, that consciousness is the eternal window of

God through which we, all mankind, look out upon this magnificent universe in all its glory and mathematical harmony. It should be further obvious that God can have absolutely no recognition for his existence and achievements unless through the consciousness of man, who is an eternal attribute of God himself. And once it is fully realized that we are the conscious expression of God who exists eternally — because there is no such thing as the past or future, only the present, which is eternal — we will become completely conscious of our own eternal life; otherwise, we will be eternal unconsciously.

The perception of these relations makes it obvious that the same general experiences we have gone through of being little boys and girls with a mother and father, growing up, getting married, raising a family in the new world, and remarking about the time way back in the olden days when man believed the earth was flat, his will free, and his eyes a sense organ, will continue throughout eternity because there is no such thing as a beginning and end since time, space, and consciousness are infinite and eternal attributes of the present.

However, when someone dies, it is true that he is gone and will never return to us because these relations are also undeniable. But God, through his infinite wisdom, by revealing what it means that man's will is not free, prevents in 90% of the cases any premature deaths by eliminating all war, crime, and other forms of hurt that gave rise to a justifiable retaliation, while endowing man with the intelligence to discover the remaining laws that will wipe away the other ten percent. In our Golden Age, the inception of which will take place very shortly, we will fall mutually in love, raise a family in complete freedom, health, wealth, and security, live to a ripe old age, and die only to be born for the same happiness again and again and again. Well, you tell me. Is God a reality and is he good?"

"This whole thing is so wonderful and fantastic; I can't find words to adequately express my feelings!"

"The full realization of what death actually is will destroy the desire to preserve corpses in cemeteries, for this is only a waste of land and the bodies of the deceased. No one will deny that it is sad to lose a loved companion, but satisfaction in preserving this unliving bit of matter can only be gotten when ignorance of the truth engenders the desire."

"I can only repeat what Charlie just said. I wish there was something I could do to help bring this world around a little faster."

"There is something you can do. If you bear in mind that the end of all war must take place just as soon as the leaders of the world understand the principles, then you can help by writing a letter to the President requesting that he investigate the knowledge in this book. When he gets enough of these letters, just in case he hasn't already analyzed this knowledge, the investigation will take place, and the transition will be officially launched.

In conclusion, however, there is one thing I would like for you to always remember — something I hope you will never forget for one second. The next time you feel like expressing your appreciation and gratitude for this new world that is about to unfold, don't thank me for pointing the way, because my will is not free. Thank God, for it was his wisdom, not mine, that guided us to this Promised Land."

POSTSCRIPT

As you know, the author passed away in 1991 at the age of 72. He was unable to bring his discovery to light during his lifetime. We are doing everything possible to preserve his work so that it doesn't get lost to future generations. He said many times that this knowledge belongs to the world. You can help in this effort by passing this book along to other interested readers who will, in turn, continue to spread the word.

Before leaving, would you kindly take a moment to give this book a positive review? The more 5-star ratings we receive, the better our chances of getting this discovery formally investigated. Once it is validated by the scientific community, it won't take long for a world of peace and brotherhood to be within our reach. Until then, I bid you adieu. May we all, one day, meet in the Golden Age.

If you are interested in learning more about the author, our website is:

www.declineandfallofallevil.com[1]

Our Facebook page is:

www.facebook.com/DeterminismandConscience[2]

Other books by Seymour Lessans:

---

1.   http://www.declineandfallofallevil.com/

2.   http://www.facebook.com/DeterminismandConscience

SEYMOUR LESSANS

The Scientific Discovery of 1961 (this was his very first attempt to transcribe his discovery into the kind of language others could comprehend; it has not been published)

Inception of the Golden Age (1962)

A New Earth (1965)

View From the Mountaintop (1969)

* The Secret (1971)

Beyond the Framework of Modern Thought (1976)

This Is An Urgent Message From A Visitor To Your Planet (1988)

Decline and Fall of All Evil: The Most Important Discovery of Our Times (A compilation by his daughter, Janis Rafael) (2015)

Did you love *The Secret*? Then you should read *A New Earth*[3] by Seymour Lessans!

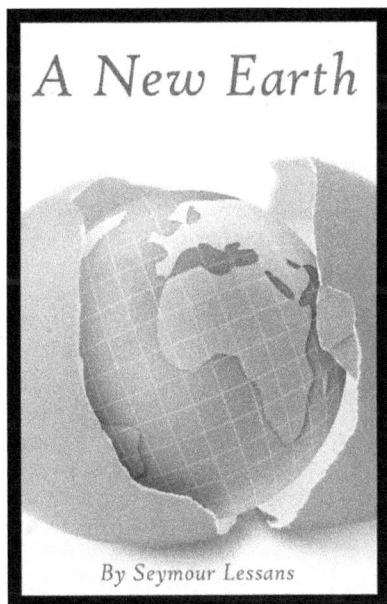

A New Earth took five years to complete. It was the author's 3rd attempt to reveal a scientific discovery that has the power to prevent war, crime, discrimination, and many other evils plaguing mankind. This knowledge reveals that the long-awaited Messiah (the solution to all our problems) is nothing other than a psychological law of man's nature which has remained undiscovered, like atomic energy, until now. By discovering this well-concealed law and demonstrating its power, a catalyst is introduced into human relations that

---

3. https://books2read.com/u/4jPxM5

4. https://books2read.com/u/4jPxM5

compelsa fantastic change in the direction our nature has been traveling. Veryfew people, when first reading the Preface, which follows, willbelieve these changes possible. However, mathematical proof isundeniably established as the text is read and understood.

Read more at www.declineandfallofallevil.com.

About the Author

Seymour Lessans was born on September 29, 1918 in Newark, New Jersey. He passed away on January 29, 1991. He was the third of four brothers. All through his life he had a tremendous thirst for knowledge, and after many years of extensive reading and careful analysis he made a discovery about the nature of man whose life will be completely revolutionized for his benefit once this discovery is recognized by science. This discovery reveals a natural law which has the power to bring about a new world (the Golden Age of man); a world without war, crime, and all the other evils plaguing mankind.

The rest of his life was devoted to reaching those who could help validate his findings, but he continued to hit stumbling blocks at every turn. His loving wife stood by his side during these difficult years knowing he had a mission to accomplish. Unfortunately, he was unable to bring his discovery to light in his lifetime as he was not a member of a leading university, and held no distinguishing titles. He could not get anyone to listen or to give him the time of day.

His family and all those who knew him will always be inspired by his courage and determination in the midst of incredible odds. His dying words were, "My day will come." He knew he wouldn't be here to see this great change, but he was comforted in the knowledge that no matter how long it took, it would just be a matter of time before this new world becomes a reality. It is with this hope in mind that his life's work (7 books in all from 1961-1988) will be recognized in the 21st century. With everyone's help, it will be possible *in our lifetime* to reach those scientists who can stamp this knowledge with the brevet of truth. This discovery is dedicated to the author, Seymour Lessans, for his incredible contribution to humanity.

Read more at www.declineandfallofallevil.com.